The Pocket

CREATIVE WRITING

First published in Great Britain 2002 by Pocket Essentials,
18 Coleswood Road, Harpenden, Herts, AL5 1EQ

Distributed in the USA by Trafalgar Square Publishing,
PO Box 257, Howe Hill Road, North Pomfret, Vermont 05053

Copyright © Neil Nixon 2002
Series Editor: Paul Duncan

A CIP catalogue record for this book is available from the British Library.

ISBN 1-904048-09-9

2 4 6 8 10 9 7 5 3 1

Book typeset by Wordsmith Solutions Ltd
Printed and bound by Cox & Wyman

For Basho [1644-1694] and Bolan [1947-1977]
They said so much in so few words.

CONTENTS

Introduction:
Pipe Dream Or Practical Subject?

'What writing is - telepathy, of course.'

Stephen King

What this book is: An introduction to creative writing. An invitation for you to become actively involved and improve your writing skills. It assumes you have an interest in writing, a willingness to hold an open mind with regard to ideas and the persistence to work your way through some exercises. This book is a complement to other activities, for example the joining of a writers group.

What this book isn't: A course in itself, a primer on the use of the English language or a guaranteed short cut to earning a fortune.

How to use this book: Work your way through the book taking time to consider each point and exercise. Be prepared to put in your own effort to further explore the issues and ideas you find most useful. Combine the use of the book with standard reference sources, such as those listed in the section at the back. Keep referring to this section and your notes from Exercise 1.

What creative writing is: An activity enjoyed by millions. A passion that offers stunning insights. A means by which some seek recognition and income and, last but not least, an academic subject, available at all levels in the UK from short-run recreational courses to Ph.D. study. All of which begs a question. Can we totally understand it? There is no simple answer. The nature of creative writing depends on what you want from the subject. This multiplicity of creative writings arises because the term lends itself as a description to a range of activities. Sometimes this occurs by default. We call something creative writing because the term itself is part of the English language. We use it to describe writing that is hard to pin down with other descriptions. For example:

* Students developing free form compositions during a GCSE programme might be told to spend fifteen minutes doing some creative writing before sharing their results with the class. This activity encourages the use of words, descriptions and imagination. All useful for raising coursework marks.

* Senior industrial managers on a training programme may produce creative writing before using their creativity as a means of identifying their thought processes. The activity aims to help managers reflect on their perceptions of the world and, therefore, their approach to managing.

* Writing workshops are popular in prison education. They allow convicts to explore ideas and possibilities in a blame-free environment. They also provide freedom and escape in a situation lacking either.

All of the above are regularly labelled as creative writing. All of these activities revolve around creative thinking and the production of writing. However, they do highlight the problem of defining the term in a simple way. The other thing we can learn from these activities is that creative writing is something often done in a controlled environment. An activity that combines creative writing with notions of focus and purpose. Creative writing is often applied to problems, like helping prisoners, because it offers the potential for useful results.

Prison education seeks to do more than offer qualifications. Prison is a space in which people can focus, think and face realities. Sometimes the production of creative work, like writing, allows the introduction of difficult ideas, like exploring a crime from a victim's point of view.

One creative writing exercise I have never seen on a creative writing course is to consider the various applications of creative writing and invent new names for them all! This is a serious point, not an ironic observation. The term 'creative writing' serves as a popular verbal shorthand amongst the population. It is as useful and vague as 'bad back,' 'bad hair day,' or 'going out.' Like these terms it has its roots in reality. People, after all, have bad backs, go out and do write creatively. The term 'creative writing' has become part of general speech because it is an easy term to use and it describes the activities to which it refers.

But the term is imprecise. The very ease of using it is the main reason for this problem. The problem often manifests itself in the way that the subject is discussed as if it is one thing or one kind of activity.

The courses on the subject alone vary enormously. At the University of East Anglia a highly-rated postgraduate course in Creative Writing has produced two Booker Prize winning students. Around the country others dabble in Creative Writing in a relaxed environment within adult education. Another example of the popularity of the term 'creative writing' regularly haunts me. I manage and deliver a course on Professional Writing in Dartford. This is a *Professional Writing* course and yet it is regularly mistaken for a *Creative Writing* course, often by my own colleagues. Some of them are well aware that we oblige students to write genuine scripts, book submissions and the like. This is not a complaint. It is an important observation we have to keep in mind if we are to understand creative writing. Consider another example. The company name of Hoover is synonymous with any machine that qualifies as a vacuum cleaner. The brand name and the activity are one and the same for many people who speak English. Despite spending a lot of money to win an important legal case against Hoover, the Dyson company are still struggling to establish their name with their cleaner. People regularly state they have a "Hoover" when they don't own any machine made by that company. The term 'creative writing' is, roughly, as ubiquitous as the Hoover name. Many people do not realise that creative writing is a multifaceted subject. It is different things to different people. The courses on offer vary. So do the jobs done by creative writers.

So, at the outset, we need to establish two things. Firstly, that creative writing is a general term for a range of activities. Secondly, that we define the purpose for the writing. Creative writing continues to expand and develop because a range of people find it purposeful. In some cases creative writing leads people to life-changing revelations. In many cases it leads people to discoveries of talent and potential for development. In most cases it remains an activity that enriches lives.

When I started interviewing potential students for undergraduate studies in writing I soon discovered it was useful to spend time attempting to talk people out of coming on a course. One point I make time and again in interviews and the early stages of the course is that being a writer resembles being an athlete or an actor. From the outside the illusion is often that success and achievement are built on talent. This illusion is often fostered by the publicity attaching itself to successful people. The reality is often different. Success is the result of consistent hard work coupled with the development of a person's own ability to understand their talent, work with it and develop a range of skills. Successful writers usually follow this pattern.

After years of teaching aspiring writers I know there is no shortage of ambition and raw talent. There is a shortage of people who can step outside of their own viewpoint long enough to see their talent as others see it. This may be more evident on a course where I am attempting to turn raw talents into employable writers but the same observations have been made by others who work with writers aiming simply to improve their skills.

This is a creative writing book. More accurately, a primer that introduces the subject and sets out ways to develop your talent and apply your skills. The book deals with practical applications of writing and the use of writing for personal development. You should find items of particular personal interest. You may find work that genuinely excites you, writers who represent useful role models or information that forms the basis of a personal plan.

Creative writing as a subject can offer you a great deal. It will offer you the most if you are honest with yourself about your aims. There is a certain irony in opening a book on a creative subject by suggesting that we impose rules and limits. But it is important to remember advice given by one writer

gest is a useful role model. For the Japanese haiku poet Matsuo
writing was, quite literally, his life. There was no real separation
n his Zen Buddhist faith, his travels, his work with his students and
h prolific writing. Basho's greatest writing was an expression of his very
soul and his last haiku, delivered to disciples as the master lay on his death-
bed, was a final affirmation of faith.

> Sick on a journey -
> over parched fields
> dreams wander on

It is a poignant work. The tired and terminally ill body of the poet pitted
against the greater reality of his work and his soul continuing their journey.
The 'dreams' in question represent both his own hopes for future existence
and the seeds of awareness sown by his poetry and developed by his students and their followers. Basho's work and teachings have been para-
phrased and translated with some variations over the years. His work and
example continue in the English language because the ideas and honesty
behind them are strong and sincere. One staple piece of wisdom he imparted
to his students is still quoted by teachers to this day: Learn all the rules, then
forget them. This is not a conundrum. Basho's belief was that rules provide
a focus and structure but never an end in themselves. His advice was
intended to give his students the ability to write within the form of the haiku
whilst maintaining the more important aspect of being true to themselves.
Basho's belief was that students taking his advice would write purposefully
and honestly. Their self-discipline from working within the rules would
assist but not stifle their creativity.

I think this is important advice at this stage of the book. Creative writing
is the most personal of subjects. The implication in the term is that the writing we do will come from our individual creativity. The danger of such a
subject is that it indulges individuals to little useful purpose. As we will see
in the later chapters, there are valid exercises in producing the most obtuse
and random writing. However, the value of having this work as an end in
itself is questionable. The danger in such situations is that we create only
words and these, in turn, simply create a feeling of emptiness in the writer.
If you recognise the feeling or the danger of that feeling called anomie, literally a lack of focus and fulfilment, I think it important to complete the exercise that closes this opening section.

Since I'm about to make demands on you and ask you to spend time
being honest with yourselves the least I can do is to be honest with you. The
ideas, exercises and examples here have been chosen by me. I've made
every effort within 35,000 words to cover a range of angles and deal with

the problems and ambitions I know to affect writing studen... subjective discipline. It is important to question all the adv... carefully about how useful each exercise is to you. It is also im... you know something of the assumptions I am making in bringing ... to you and something of what I bring to the subject.

I'm a writer. This much I can say with certainty. I spend a substantial part of each week writing. I also spend large amounts of time thinking up ideas. I get paid for my work and paid for teaching others to write. I don't believe that you become a writer simply by getting paid for your work. Some of my favourites amongst my own work are the books and scripts that earned me the least money. The major difference between getting paid and not getting paid is that the money tends to simplify the debate about whether or not someone is a writer. There are differing opinions amongst writers about just what it means to be a writer. So I should be honest about the assumptions that went into this book. These are my assumptions, make of them what you will.

I believe writers are made, not born. I think it certain that our backgrounds and the events that surround us contribute to make us writers. A good example of this is, I believe, the vivid and reflective young men who made up the war poets of World War 1. The collision of their youthful and often naïve perceptions and the almost indescribable horrors they saw produced work that has lost none of its power almost a century later. Consider Wilfred Owen's description of the victim of a gas attack.

> If in some smothering dreams, you too could pace behind the
> wagon that we flung him in,
> And watch the white eyes writhing in his face,
> His hanging face, like a devil's sick of sin,
> If you could hear at every jolt, the blood come
> Come gurgling from froth-corrupted lungs
> Bitter as the cud [2]

This is an extreme example. I don't suggest putting your life in danger for the sake of writing. Put simply, we need to be open enough to see our surroundings and the events of our lives for what they are - the raw material for writing and the events that make us into writers. I think that honesty about yourself and what you bring to this work is a vital quality at the outset. It is also the hardest quality to isolate. Tricks and traits in your writing are valuable. An awareness of why you are writing is invaluable.

I don't believe that creative writing is totally separable from the writer. That is why that final haiku of Basho is my favourite poem. It is not so

.n a poem about him as a poem of him. And, within sight of his own death, he had every opportunity to forsake writing.

Some other beliefs that have underpinned this book and my own writing work revolve around the approach I have taken. I realised some time ago that some writers simply throw themselves into projects. They do not spend a long time working on ideas. This spontaneous and instinctive approach soon worked for me. I'm not suggesting you should be completely impulsive. I still plot, outline, revise and rewrite complex pieces of work like books and scripts. But, I'm very much of the opinion that uncertainty and experimentation are useful. I deliberately seek out work that will put new demands on me and pitch me into new areas. I think shutting up and putting up is a valuable learning experience.

I differ from some writing teachers because I am by no means a purist when it comes to literature. This much will be obvious by the time you've encountered examples including the work of Bill Hicks, Rebecca Ray, Stanley Manly and the scriptwriters of *Coronation Street*. These are not people generally featured in books on creative writing. My own view is that anyone who uses language or ideas in a creative and striking way may have something to teach us. I've selected examples to make points, not because a vast body of critical literature recognises all these examples as important. I have not cast this book in my own image but it is important that you are aware of the areas in which I may be biased. Feel free to disagree. I want you to question, experiment and make your own decisions. My major aim in this is to help you find your own voice as a writer. [3]

This book is built around the main themes of creative writing. It includes sections and exercises based on many staple items from creative writing courses - work that has helped a diverse range of writers to realise their talent and make discoveries about themselves. Which brings us to the final point before we start to itemise and explore creative writing. This introduction has combined the topic areas that make up creative writing, the uses to which this activity can be put and my own opinions. But the context of creative writing is not the subject of this book. My own importance to the whole thing is marginal. If this book is to work properly you need to realise that the information, exercises and author are the background here. I may have written the words, but this book is about you!

So, now it's your turn:

You will need a clean sheet of paper, preferably a note pad with the facility to rip off the sheets and file them. Write answers to the following questions. Keep them safe and remind yourself of your opinions when you are working through the exercises in the rest of the book.

Exercise 1

There are no right or wrong answers to any of the questions below. The purpose of the exercise is to give you a focus before you start working through the book. If you were in a group or starting a course you would realise on completion of this exercise that there were others around who shared some of your ambitions, talents and experience. You would also find writers whose whole approach and reasons for writing were very different to your own. You would soon realise that, despite the differences, you shared many of the same needs.

Answer the following questions as honestly as you can. If you find any question particularly hard, leave it for a while and return to it. You may even want to ask the opinion of someone whose judgement you trust.

1: State, as honestly as you can, why you want to write.

2: Identify three useful skills you bring to your writing, for example an ability to understand character, a strong work ethic, a sharp sense of humour. These do not have to be writing skills. Motivation is as important as talent. Simply focus on three things you do well which may help in your writing.

3: In three to five sentences, describe your most enjoyable experience as a writer. Briefly explain what made the experience so enjoyable.

4: In three and five sentences, describe your least enjoyable experience as a writer. Explain what made the experience so negative.

5: On a scale of 1 to 10 in which 1 indicates no ambition and 10 indicates high ambition, rate the following statements.

As a writer, I want to:

> Produce artistic and creative work.
> Make money.
> Be famous.
> Work exclusively with my own ideas.
> Achieve results quickly.
> Work very hard to perfect my skills.
> Write scripts.
> Write non-fiction books.
> Write fictional books.
> Write poetry.
> Write for television and radio.
> Write drama.
> Use my writing to discover more about myself.
> Avoid discovering more about myself.

13

6: On a scale of 1 to 10, in which 1 indicates a strong No and 10 indicates a strong Yes, rate the following three statements.

I find it easy to take constructive criticism on my writing.
I feel confident in my own ability to face a range of challenges as a writer.
Writing is the most important interest I have.

7: Finally, is there any important aspect of your writing or the reasons for writing that you have been unable to include in the answers to this exercise. If so, make a note about it now.

Look over your answers and double-check that they are as accurate as possible. File them for future reference.

These answers should provide you with two important areas of input as you work through this book. Firstly, they should serve as a regular reminder of your own areas of interest, allowing you to keep a distance and objectivity throughout the chapters on specific subjects. This may work in two ways. Firstly, if you are clear on your objectives for writing you are more likely to be able to decide on the importance of each activity and each chapter. For example, if you have little interest in making money as a writer then you can treat the material devoted to this subject as an interesting diversion. The information and exercises may be entertaining but don't feel bad about lacking the motivation to follow the advice. Secondly, the answers you have should provide you with a means to gauge your progress. In some cases this may involve improved skills and awareness leading you to revise your ideas. In other cases you may find yourself thinking reflectively about particular choices and changing your opinions.

At this stage I want to make one observation and three suggestions.

This is a book about you. Therefore, you are in charge and you are free to get as involved as you want at each stage.

I suggest you attempt every exercise and take every chapter in the spirit intended. This is a spirit of open enquiry, presenting you with material and ideas that should help you improve your skills and awareness as a writer.

I suggest that hard work and a willingness to suspend any preconceived ideas will be useful to you whilst working through the book.

I also suggest that being over-critical of yourself is to be avoided at all costs. This will stifle creativity and your own distinctive voice as a writer.

You may have noted the quote at the opening of the chapter. "What writing is - Telepathy, of course." This is taken out of context but I feel it important to explain the quote at this stage. It opens a chapter entitled 'What Writing Is,' in Stephen King's book *On Writing*. [4] King's point is straightforward. Writing is an effective means of transmitting specific thoughts over time and distance. Writers long dead can still live in our conscious minds. King's point about the power of writing is based around his own work as a consistently popular fiction writer. His examples revolve around storytellers.

I'd like to add one further consideration. Creative writing often involves a contact with your self and your own ideas. These are ideas that are hard to explain and sometimes hard to hold in your mind. Creative writing is a means to discover yourself. In effect you can discover yourself as a writer and thinker much as you discover the work of others. None of which negates the notion that writing is telepathy. Telepathy is literally 'supposed communication by means other than the senses.' [5] The traditional view of telepathy may involve communication between minds but it does not rule out self-revelation or intra-personal communication. Handled with an open mind and spirit of enquiry, creative writing is a vital and important channel that allows you to communicate with the deep and dark corners of your mind. It is no accident that writing activities remain popular in areas of study devoted to self-discovery. As mentioned earlier, prisoners being faced with the implications of their actions and high-powered managers attempting to analyse their own management strategies may use creative writing as a means to self-discovery. If it works for them, there is a chance of it providing a similar insight for you. On a simpler level there is every chance it will provide you with the means to communicate more effectively, express ideas, explore feelings and experiences and find creative fulfilment.

So, we are ready to explore the areas of creative writing, to help you enhance the skills and ideas you bring to the subject. Pipe dream or practical subject? Creative writing is what you make it.

1. Seeds

'Anyone who has survived an average childhood has enough to
write about for a dozen years.'

Flannery O'Connor

One strange thing about writing is that many people find themselves
bursting with ideas when they are driving the car, doing the shopping or settling down to sleep. Faced with a blank page and two hours of free time the
same people can find themselves unable to write anything coherent. Every
single word seems to bring new depths of self-doubt. The time to write, at
first so precious, turns into a torture session.

It's a situation I've heard described by many writers. One form of the
infamous writer's block. If you've experienced that situation it may be a
comfort to know that many of the great and the good share your trouble.
Douglas Adams, most famous as the author of *The Hitchhikers Guide To
The Galaxy* and its sequels, was one famous sufferer. Several of his friends
noted that Douglas Adams had a whole string of avoidance activities.
Everything from a long phone conversation to fussing over making a perfect
cup of tea served to take up time, getting him away from the task of writing
another side-splitting best-seller.

The important lesson here is that getting started can be nerve-wracking,
even for the most successful writers. You, and you alone, should be making
the final decisions about what you write and when you write. This chapter is
devoted to making it possible for you to write effectively, whatever the subject, style or audience.

In the previous chapter, I noted that being a writer resembles being an
athlete or an actor. Many have a basic talent, a great number can imitate
some of the performance of a professional, few can emulate such perfor-
mances. The distance between ambition and achievement may partly be
explained by luck, but most of it is hard work. Most of the hard work that
turns amateurs into household names is work devoted to a purpose that
makes sense to the person in question. There are many examples we could
choose. Not all of them writers. I'd like to mention three because each
shows us something important about developing your own work. Galileo,
the inventor of the telescope, was hounded as a heretic because he suggested
that the Earth wasn't the centre of universe. His calculations and observations told him he was right. Galileo knew that he was smarter than his critics
and that he had something important to say.

Many people in the early 1970s were astounded to see Marc Bolan and T.Rex emerge as the first major British post-Beatles pop sensation. Bolan had been seen a few years previously, cross-legged and warbling with an acoustic guitar. By the early 1970s he was re-invented as a strutting, preening rock god with a stack of chart-topping singles and albums to his credit. Some dubbed him a "sell-out," and many simply didn't understand the change. In reality the progression in his work was clear. From the earliest days some of the themes in his writing, like the use of images based around cars, were evident. So was the debt he owed to early rockers like Eddie Cochran. The apparent gulf between his early recordings and huge hits wasn't really that wide. Marc Bolan found his voice and built on his interests and ideas. As a writer and performer he remained alert to possibilities of market and creativity, and used the tools of his trade, like words, riffs and clothes, to achieve his goals. Once again, he was probably smarter than many of his critics and he retained a love for his work and a sense of his own creative power for most of his career. Probably not something he could have achieved so easily had he consistently listened to others who told him what he should have been doing. He is now respected as a pop innovator. Respect based largely on work savaged by earlier critics.

The final example is known by most cherishing notions of a writing career. JK Rowling wrote in a coffee bar with her baby daughter asleep beside her. Short of money, struggling as a single parent, she worked hard to write a book that would sell itself to a publisher as a popular work. Publishers, including the massive HarperCollins, turned down the book but *Harry Potter And The Philosopher's Stone* started the most exciting literary cult that book publishing had seen in decades. JK Rowling's success is incredible. Her example proves that ambitions as a writer can be achieved on the back of a well-developed idea. You don't need to know anyone in the publishing world. You don't need a huge track record of writing.

You are also well advised to consider the quote from Flannery O'Connor that opens this chapter. Whatever your situation in life, you already have enough material to become a regular writer. If you want to, a regular and paid writer. Anything is possible. What you achieve will be based on your own decisions and the work you are prepared to apply to the task.

Just Do It

A slogan that served the Nike sports empire so successfully is a fitting place to start considering flexing your own writing muscles. 'Just do it' sold Nike trainers and T-shirts because it suggested there was a power and attitude in every individual that could find an outlet in active sports. The clothing and shoes were one manifestation of buying into that reality.

'Just do it' is an advertising slogan, a useful motto and also an example of creative writing. In fact, wherever you look there are ideas, examples and events that can help you to start writing. Seizure and inactivity in the face of a blank page or computer screen are avoidable. The cure for the condition involves a belief in your own power and a sense of your own purpose. You can 'Just do' writing as easily as you can just do running.

Starting from scratch it is advisable to establish a few parameters. Your first priority is to get writing. Your second priority is to discover a range of things you can achieve as a writer. At this stage, nothing else matters. So forget about writing a successful script or blockbuster novel. Forget about impressing your parents, shocking your friends or matching the level of angst and insight you've loved for all those years on your Spiritualized albums. Know only that you will write and that these first steps are about freeing your creativity. Once you know you can write you can worry about channelling your skills.

The exercises in this chapter are a useful start. The advice that precedes them represents some of the common ground between a range of writing courses. Writers and teachers of writing are agreed that the following are important:

Reading: More specifically, reading, watching and listening widely. It is vital you are open to the influence of anyone using words effectively. It is a mistake for any writer to root themselves in one area of work to the extent that they discount skills and insights on offer from reading widely. As the workforce of the western world has become more likely to change careers and update its abilities phrases like 'transferable skills' have become widely used. Writing skills are transferable. This is true for professional and recreational writers. Writers across a range of disciplines need the same abilities. The ability to deliver a succinct phrase may be the backbone of a well-constructed novel. It is a skill you could improve by studying inventive greetings cards, comic strips and adverts. Characterisation may be central to a major drama for stage or radio. It is also central to this paraphrasing of the opening of the act of comedian Bill Hicks:

"Aah! I'm tired right now, real tired. Tired of doing comedy, tired of travelling. Tired of staring out at your blank faces every night. Tired of trying to bring little gems of comedy into your lives. Thoughts you couldn't invent for yourselves... So, hi, how are ya?!... I'm really glad to be here. I'm always glad to be here, wherever I am." [1]

Hicks' comedy continues to have a cult following long after his death. He remains valued as a performer who combined an unashamed awareness of his own intelligence with the ability to tell the truth. This introduction is heavily ironic and an indication of the character that Hicks brought to his work. Superficially, Hicks seems to insult his audience. Nothing could be further from the truth. Hicks' crowd prided themselves on being intelligent and self-aware. The comedian establishes inside a minute that he is aware that his audience can see through empty platitudes. Having identified himself as reflective and honest, he can get on with the serious business of making people laugh. Anyone wishing to use a dramatic character to gradually reveal serious points could learn from the ways stand-up comedians develop and present their personalities. Bill Hicks and a classic drama on Radio 4 might not share the same audience, but their character-based work shares much in terms of creative skills and planning.

Exercise 2

Read, regularly and with some sense of purpose. If you have plenty of time, devour a range of reading material. If you don't, use your time and effort as effectively as possible. The exercises below take account of the problem of limited time. Depending on the time you can usefully devote to this task, attempt one or both of these reading and listening activities:

Reading Activity 1: Set yourself the target of reading one thing per day that is outside your interest and experience. Twenty potential items are listed below. You can easily add to this list. As you read these items you should make notes on any striking aspects of language or content. You should aim to be as open minded as possible. At this stage you should simply record the details and file interesting items for future reference. The point of this exercise is to open your awareness to uses of language and the voices of writers you would normally block out. For example, reading an assignment written by someone else on a course you don't follow presents a digest of a subject written by someone aiming for an understanding. It should present a mixture of that person's writing voice and hard information. As such, it should also present you with an insight into the writer. Grammatical tricks and inventive uses of language abound in some of the other areas mentioned, like dance music and direct mail advertising. Considered from the point of view of the words they use, they provide insights that can be applied in your work. For example, dance music words and the names of dance acts play up values of community and belonging and do so in a way that re-invents the English language. The names of the acts use words like 'Crew' to give a sense of community. Many other names are self-mythologising. The Artful Dodger is a dance act who shares his name with a Dickens character and, allegedly, built his own name on his ability to lift sounds from the records of others and disguise them so well that the original performers couldn't spot their work. His name re-invents an old literary image and mythologises his achievements. Knowing the facts behind the information at this stage is not important. The point is to open yourself up to aspects of language use that currently elude you.

Items to read:

Safety information leaflets relating to your work or interests.
Internet information on an obscure medical condition.
Local paper obituaries. (see below)
Estate agents' descriptions of properties you don't intend buying.
Internet chat room or fan forum information on musical acts, famous actors or sports stars of no interest to you.
The next 10 pieces of junk mail to arrive in your home.
An assignment written for a course you are not following.
The copy describing goods and services in *Yellow Pages* entries.
Lyrics to a dance hit.
Lyrics to a novelty pop song.
Lyrics to a song that was a hit in another country but sold poorly in the UK.
The headlines, but not the articles, in a broadsheet paper.
The headlines, but not the articles, in a tabloid paper.
The collected work of a haiku poet or poets.
A themed anthology of poetry.
The names of acts on sale in a dance music shop.
The opening chapter from a Mills and Boon novel.
The opening chapter from a non-fiction book on a subject of little interest to you.
A bath book for very young children.
The copy from the next 20 advertising billboards you see.

Consider the following example, drawn from local paper obituaries. The following obituaries appeared in *Downs Mail*, a local monthly paper covering part of Maidstone and part of the Weald Of Kent.

Frobisher's Manageress

Jennie Keatley, 47, of Bluett St suffered a short illness and died suddenly. She was well known to local people after her years of working for Frobisher's where she rose to become manager. Many corporate and regular customers from Frobisher's joined friends and family in a packed service at Vinters Park Crematorium. Jennie leaves husband John and daughters Lucy and Lynsey.

Former Detling Parish Clerk

Tom Atkinson, 92, of Marple Lane, Detling, died in his sleep at Maidstone Hospital on November 2nd, having been ill for two years. A popular and well-known figure in the village, Tom's involvement in local life included a 12-year spell as clerk to Detling Parish Council where his duties included acting as secretary and treasurer to the Village Hall Management Committee. He also served The Detling Society as secretary for many years. His wife, Martha, told *Downs Mail* "Tom was involved in most of the things that were going on in Detling for many years."

Tom and Austrian-born Martha met at the end of World War 2 when he was a member of the Royal Leicester Regiment. He returned to enjoy a 48-year career in public service culminating in running a department for the GLC from which he retired in the mid-1970s.

Tom's many talents included a conversational and reading familiarity with French, German and Russian. He was also a keen musician and music fan. He leaves wife Martha, daughters Renata, Simona and Edwina and four grandchildren. [2]

Discussion of the example: *Downs Mail* is restrained and informative in its obituaries. It emphasises facts and significant details in a brief and punchy manner. The editor describes the obituaries section as "a busy page." Busy in this sense means using general, descriptive words to summarise complex areas of life. Brief descriptions of complex facts are common. For example, Tom Atkinson was a 'member' of a regiment. There are no further details of his military career. Jennie Keatley 'rose' to become a manager. Tom Atkinson was 'popular and well known.' Tom also returned from army service to 'enjoy' a 48-year career and a few of his 'many talents' are listed at the end of the entry. There are sound business reasons for local papers taking such a restrained approach to their work. Limited space and the need to keep a wide range of advertisers happy are foremost amongst these. At first glance this often leaves the copy in such publications looking bland. From the point of creative writing there are things to be learned. The rapid sketching of the characters does leave a busy feeling to the writing. This approach works well in fact and fiction. Many writers have to fight the temptation to add details of every event in their work. A close look at the economy and discipline in popular and local journalism shows that it is possible to sketch characters and situations with economy. The same approaches have been used successfully by highly-respected and very creative writers. Ernest Hemingway wrote with great economy, letting the characters and situations draw readers into his work and often leaving out the tiny details to let the clarity of his work make important points. The Irish writer Roddy Doyle has employed the same approach, notably in *Paddy Clarke Ha Ha Ha*. This work explores the world through the eyes of a mischievous and lively ten-year-old boy. Characters are frequently drawn in a sketchy manner, as a ten-year-old might view adults. In the book Paddy Clarke lacks the insight into the adult world to make complete sense of events like the arguments between his parents. The consistent economy of the language and Doyle's busy approach to the narrative eventually build a compelling portrait of Paddy's life. It's a viewpoint perhaps best represented in the breathless audio version of the book. [3] This example proves that work with huge ambitions can be built on the simplest use of language. Reading brief and less ambitious work, like local journalism, can provide an insight into an effective writing style.

Reading Activity 2: Gather half a dozen pen portraits from a range of sources. These are short, punchy descriptions of people and their achievements. This activity may include some listening in place of reading. Ensure that the sources vary and that they are unlikely to appeal to the same readers. A list of potential sources is included below. Gather all of these pen portraits together and then take time to imagine scenarios in which two of these people meet. These scenarios should be mundane and should not be built into stories. This is an exercise in reading and reflecting. Let your mind wander. You do not have to write down a story for your characters. You should aim to imagine exchanges of dialogue between them. To try and hear them speak and imagine their reactions. For example, place two of the characters in a cafe. One is a waiter/waitress, the other is trying to decide between two items on the menu. How would the discussion develop? How, for example, does someone in the throes of a mental torture as deep as Hamlet's dilemma order a coffee? How do they cope with the fact that something listed on the menu is not available?

The exercise might seem strange at first, especially since it obliges you to imagine fragments of story and avoid building a narrative. Fight any instinct you might have to treat it as a joke. This exercise has two highly useful elements. Firstly, the concentration on reading means your ideas are not being put up to public test at this stage. Secondly, it forces you away from characters you already know and obliges you to react to newly-discovered characters. You are then obliged to think laterally and develop imaginative possibilities. The skills required to achieve results in this exercise are the bedrock of creative writing. So approach the exercise with an open mind and sense of honesty. It is worth the effort.

Sources of pen portraits:

> Short items in tabloid papers featuring people who aren't famous.
> Author biographies from your own bookshelf. (See below)
> Descriptions of people from a brochure advertising a company.
> Obituaries from national papers devoted to eminent people you know nothing about.
> An overheard conversation in a public place in which one person you don't know describes him/herself to another. (See below)
> Descriptions of people from their own personal websites.
> The lyrics to a song in which a singer appears to be describing themselves.
> A soliloquy from a play in which a character debates a decision. [4]
> The opening description with which a character is introduced in a book.
> The funniest piece of self-description you've ever heard from a child.
> Film dialogue in which one character provides a short description of another.
> The opening lines of a stand-up comedian's introduction of themselves.
> Liner notes about a musical performer from a CD.
> Text introductions to computer game characters from inserts with the game or the game itself.

Consider the following examples. I decided when I started writing this section to include an author biography and an overheard conversation. I took the most convenient examples of each once the section was complete:

Author biographies: The closest book to my computer as I wrote this section was Davis Miller's *The Tao Of Muhammad Ali*. It contains two separate descriptions of the author:

> Davis Miller was a sickly 12-year-old child when he first encountered Ali. From this meeting there developed a powerful relationship that has lasted thirty years. *The Tao Of Muhammad Ali* is a unique portrait of this exceptional fighter, and a compelling story of hero worship, of fathers and sons, of strength through wisdom.

and

> Davis Miller's writing has appeared in *Rolling Stone*, *Men's Journal*, *Esquire*, *Sport* magazine, *Sports Illustrated* and numerous other periodicals. His first published story 'My Dinner With Ali' was voted by the Sunday Magazine Editors Association to be the best essay published in a newspaper magazine in the US in 1989. His story 'The Zen Of Muhammad Ali' was nominated for the 1994 Pulitzer Prize for feature writing; that piece was later included in the 1994 edition of *The Best American Sports Writing*. Davis Miller has two children, Joanna and Isaac, and lives near Wiston-Salem, North Carolina. [5]

An overheard conversation:

The following conversation was the most recent addition to my notes before writing this section of the book. It involved two visitors to North West Kent College. I have no idea who they were or what purpose brought them to the College. Both wore suits and appeared to be involved in inspecting or advising our management. As they signed out of the building one commented to the other on his dislike of straying too far from London. The lines were delivered in a South London accent. An accent that pronounces South London as "Sarf" London.

> "I like to be back in the city. Y'know, where you can hear traffic and police sirens and people and that at night. I don't like it out in the country. All you can hear there at night is animals tearing each other apart."

I had a coffee, took the notes on Davis Miller and the anonymous College visitor, and considered placing the characters together. The first thing that struck me was the massive gulf in their thinking. Davis Miller appears to search for depth and meaning. The suggestion of his building a lasting relationship with Ali, his award and his nomination for other honours all present a portrait of a man looking beneath the surface. The notion of 'strength through wisdom' attaches to his life and work. By contrast, the college visitor appears to search for certainty when faced with the unfamiliar.

One obvious scenario in which the characters could meet would be a sports event. Miller's sports writing might take him to London. The other character appears allergic to life far beyond the fringes of London. I pictured them in a long snaking queue for food between bouts at a boxing night. I imagined a conversation starting when the College visitor overheard Miller's accent. I could hear exchanges between them on a number of points. In terms of boxing, I could imagine the Londoner talking up the chances of uncomplicated clubbing fighters on the bill, putting his thoughts into phrases like "He'll drop 'im inside two rounds, no bother." Perhaps the Londoner would have claimed an insight into the better hard punchers of the last twenty years. "Old Frank Bruno, right, people say he hadn't no skill. But I'm tellin' ya, he hit harder than anyone I ever saw. Shame about his glass chin and that cos he coulda' been one of the greatest ever if he took a punch a bit better."

Against the certainties of the Londoner Davis Miller might shrug and speak more quietly. Starting by throwing back platitudes, "Yeah, right," before starting his own verbal sparring, relying on an inside knowledge of fighters and their skills gathered through his journalism. A turning point in such a conversation could be a comment about a boxer from Miller. "Bruno, he was never so mobile you know. He always got caught by a fighter with good movement around the ring." And so on. The two characters began building fragments of dialogue in my mind. The possibilities started to present themselves. Then again, I was drinking some suicidally strong coffee!

So with a little thought randomly gathered characters can begin to live and breathe in your mind. Their accents, their appearance, the comments they make and a few biographical details might be the starting point. The end result is your creative imagination working in a way that does not require a definite story structure or an existing opinion to channel it.

A final note on the reading exercises: One of the main objections I've heard from students concerning the reading load attached to a writing course is the obligation they feel to devote time to an activity that produces no writing. I understand the problem. I've maintained a writing career against the competing demands of bringing up a family, holding down another job and fitting in anything else that matters. But the exercises above are designed to provide results in very limited time. They are also designed to start a thought process and awareness of source material that can be directed into a range of other writing tasks. If you have time to read a range of books, magazines, papers and websites that is fine. If not, the above exercises will still provide you with a range of insights into character and your own creative imagination.

Taking notes: This activity makes a natural extension from the reading and listening outlined above. Looking and listening are central to note-taking. Different writers have their own methods of gathering information. At this stage what matters most is making the recording and collecting of information a central part of your writing. The means you choose might involve tape or mini disc recorders, notebooks or even a sketch pad.

It is important to be open to a range of influences. The point about note-taking is that you are never totally away from writing and this, in turn, should sharpen your awareness to material you normally ignore. In general, people spend days working towards the next event, aware of the present and thinking about the future. This means we ignore much of the behaviour and events surrounding us. More accurately, we see them but choose to disregard them. A notepad and a little time can provide a means of mining a rich supply of material. The things you should note are people's turns of phrase, their odd habits and the situations you encounter. All can supply character and colour for your writing.

John Cleese based the character of Basil Fawlty on a real hotelier. Most writers, however far-fetched their work, root it in reality. Terry Pratchett is a leading pioneer of the genre of comedy fantasy. His success reached such a level that one in every fifty books sold by WH Smiths was a Pratchett title. The action in his best-selling Discworld novels takes place in a huge flat world on the back of giant turtle. Despite this, his observations and awareness of everyday characters make Discworld a believable place.

Caroline Aherne, famous for the *Mrs Merton* and *Royle Family* television shows is another writer with a track record of pulling phrases and observations from everyday life. Much of the humour in the pensioner chat show host Mrs Merton came from a blend of scripted comedy and the well-observed mannerisms of a well-meaning but blinkered character, trapped in her own time and values. This was best demonstrated in single lines. She once asked the alcoholic former footballer George Best if it was all the running around that had made him so thirsty!

It might have been scripted comedy but it is also something you can note down if you go to places where different generations mingle. Where collisions of values and attitudes are inevitable. Places like bus stations. The competition for the best seats is one place where misunderstandings can develop and you can observe characters in action. The skilful and seemingly unconscious movements in queues as they wait for buses are a good first observation for note-taking writers. You might pass such a scene every day, thinking that little is happening. Place yourself to watch and you could see a great deal. Only the truly perverse and young children actually enjoy the experience of uncertainty waiting for a bus. A late bus is an annoyance because it reminds people of their powerlessness. Bus stations and stops have to be large enough to allow buses to stop, dooming them to be open to the elements. Likely to leave people stifling in summer and wind-blown in winter. Most people waiting for a bus are already thinking of being somewhere else. Often they are acutely aware of their own discomfort.

Now consider the social dimension. Polite and well-organised people are likely to turn up on time for a bus. Impulsive, disorganised and stroppy individuals are often the last to a queue. Add to this the age of people in such a situation. Groups of youngsters mingle with their grandparents' generation. Each group often hold different view of acceptable manners and behaviour. From a distance you may observe a few movements. You might notice people looking around, directing a quick glance at those in the queue they regard as threatening. These slight movements carry a wealth of information. They link to the bigger issues outlined earlier.

Observation and note-taking are important skills that develop with practice. At first it is tempting to read meanings into situations as you make notes. Try to include activities that are unfamiliar to you amongst your first attempts at observation and note-taking. You can also set up a situation in which you are observing and taking notes on unfamiliar aspects of a familiar scene. Both possible approaches are covered in the exercises below.

Exercise 3

Take notes in a situation you have planned for yourself. Set times for taking notes. Concentrate on gathering information without pre-judging the value of anything you note down. Attempt one or both of the following exercises:

Note-taking exercise 1:

Observe people and their behaviour in a situation likely to produce tension and spontaneity. Concentrate on aspects of the observation that can be described in fragments of prose and write only fragments of prose. Concentrate on specific details. For example, write four or five sentences on the way different people push supermarket trolleys. Don't try to build any of this work into longer narratives at this stage. Concentrate on building descriptive phrases into your work. Repeat the exercise a number of times in different situations to ensure that you cover a range of character and situation.

Ten useful note-taking venues are outlined below. You can, of course, substitute your own ideas.

i: Place yourself in a car outside a chip shop that has a large glass window. Observe the way people move as they arrive and wait. Build in details of the smell of the shop. Does the time of year and the weather make a difference to how you relate to that smell?

ii: Find a place on a bench or in a cafe where you can observe bus queues at a busy time. Concentrate on the way that people move and how their movements communicate tension or other emotional states.

iii: Watch a group of people of very different levels of ability dancing. A class or a gathering like a wedding provide perfect opportunities. Concentrate on recording the movements of a good dancer and a poor dancer. Try to convey their ability in the description without using words that state outright whether a dancer is good or poor.

iv: Go to a park bench at a busy time. Pick a range of people and animals you can see and build a noted recording of each.

v: Find a comfortable place in a supermarket cafe and concentrate on aspects of what you see. Pick one type of behaviour, like waiting at the checkout, and use description to explore the variety of approaches you see in this one activity. Concentrate on one product at the end of every aisle visible to you. Set yourself the task of recording each item in exactly fifty words of notes.

vi: Watch a film on video in which you have little interest. Turn down the sound. Freeze frame an event in an action sequence and reconstruct the event in note form. Do the same with a close-up of the face of one character.

vii: Take an everyday item like a ten pound note or a postage stamp. Set yourself the task of recording as many different details as you can see in exactly 100 words.

viii: Visit a museum or art gallery. Choose ten exhibits and record them in exactly fifty words. Do not use their names or any details of their function. Record them entirely in terms of what you see, for example the way the light falls on them, their surface texture, their shape and size.

ix: Find a location where you can hear a range of sounds and no conversation, for example a quiet stretch of shoreline, a wood, your own bedroom with the door closed. Close your eyes and concentrate on what you can hear. Pick five sounds and record the qualities of each in less than 100 words.

x: Record four or five stages of a very mundane activity, for example making a cup of tea. Find time to do this activity on your own and pause a few times to record each stage in notes. Limit each section of notes to exactly 100 words.

Note-taking exercise 2:

Set out to take notes on an aspect of a situation. Place yourself in some vantage point offering a view of people or places. Concentrate on one aspect of the situation to the exclusion of all others. You could use one of the suggestions below. Take notes against a predetermined time. Ten minutes is a useful start. Split the note-taking time as follows:

First half, concentrating on only what you can see. Recording only aspects of description.

Second half, considering your first thoughts and impressions of what you have just noticed. Recording these and not attempting to build them into any specific structure such as a story.

Suggested note-taking situations:

i: Town or city cafe. Concentrate on one of the following:

- Walls

- Clothing

- Faces

ii: Countryside. Concentrate on one of the following:

- Grasses

- The sky

Note on the note-taking exercises: These exercises may seem strange at first. They make you more aware of detail. The focus on one aspect of what you see and the discipline of the time constraints are useful. They help you to develop a methodical and perceptive approach to your craft. This helps to turn good ideas into vivid and individual pieces of work.

A good example of this is the acclaimed debut novel from Rebecca Ray, *A Certain Age*. The book follows the gradual slide of a teenage girl into confusion and self-harm. Her life revolves around a family in which her younger brother is favoured, her parents fail to communicate effectively with each other and the main character is left watching and reflecting. Even the major incidents in her life, like losing her virginity to a much older man and the start of her self-harming, are presented as descriptions. The observations and images carry the meaning. The noted details in the book give the whole work a sense of a search for order and meaning seen from the point of view of a character who hasn't the maturity to achieve either. Readers are left to draw their own conclusions about the influence of others, like the girl's parents and boyfriend, in her situation. All aspects of her story have an observational quality, the kind of approach that can be built on good note-taking.

The character introduces herself and presents herself against other characters at school. Aside from the main character, one of the first people we meet is Holly.

> Holly was perfect. Long, slim legs, big tits, big mouth; eyes. Everything was big except her arse.

Soon she is comparing herself to Holly, especially in terms of her ability to get noticed by boys.

> I never would be like Holly, so I had to find another way of getting along. I had to let them feel me up... .I got to be sought after in a funny, dirty kind of way. I got the wolf whistles and the stares. Because I wanted them. And because I wasn't the kind of girl you had to like. I was the kind of girl you fucked.

As we first find out about the girl's home the same attention to detail sets the scene.

> I tried to think through other people's houses, work out where the difference lay. Like the newspapers, maybe. Mum keeps those in the porch as well. Hundreds of them, mostly *The Guardian* and *Hello!* Lying on the floor, discarded like that always makes me think it should be called *Goodbye!*

Dawn, the daughter of a friend of her father's, joins the school. The main character knows this is coming and worries about whether the new arrival will mess up her existing friendships.

> It was worse than I could have imagined really, and I'd tried not to imagine anything. She was wearing a black T-shirt, very baggy, so she looked like a boy. Which was funny really because the guy on the T-shirt looked like a girl. [6]

A Certain Age is a novel. As such it requires a plot and some sense of the character's motivation. But the compelling and individual voice of the character depends very much on the consistent presentation of detail. From the specifics of the porch full of papers to the clothes worn by Dawn on her first day at her new school, *A Certain Age* is built on the identification and organisation of detail. The identification with the character is all the stronger because she presents details and doesn't tell us what to think. Her place amongst the girls at school is presented in this way. We don't get a long description of the thoughts that led to her deciding to let boys feel her up. We get noted details of the wolf whistles and stares and a sense that these details set her apart. The language use is direct and honest, as we might expect with a young girl looking at her own life, 'I was the kind of girl you fucked.' These noted details coupled with the sense of order imposed by the writer paint a picture that anyone with their own memories of school might recognise. The conclusions are ours.

In life it is often small details that set people and places apart from others. A good description of a sky might be the defining moment of a story set on a Scottish Island in winter or in the heart of Ethiopia, but the two skies might be very different. The important details might concern the way a cloud moves or the curious static dust haze that hangs in the very hottest parts of Africa. Presenting these accurately is easier once you have the skills of observation and recording that start with disciplined exercises in concentration and note-taking.

Write Now: In the Hollywood comedy *Throw Momma From The Train* Billy Crystal and Danny De Vito are, respectively, a teacher and student of creative writing. The film goes for lightweight laughs rather than any heavy insight into the process of creative writing but with the accessible strength of good Hollywood dialogue the fictional teacher makes one point repeatedly. His mantra, repeated to his students, is "A writer writes, always." Not exactly good grammar. Beyond doubt as good advice.

Writing is a process that improves with practice. We don't need to trouble ourselves here with the workings of the human brain or the various ego states identified by mental health professionals. However, should you decide to study these areas you will find that the following simplistic overview is true.

The formation and articulation of thoughts through language is a process that does improve with practice. The regular use of the areas of the brain devoted to reflective thinking and language formation will allow a writer to find a consistent pace of work. More importantly, it will allow for the skills of writing to become reliable. The ability to focus and articulate is important to sound mental health. Blocked and unacknowledged emotions, especially anger and depression, can be dangerous to our mental and physical health.

Creative writing will not ensure your continued health and sanity. Used properly, it may help in this regard. At the opening stage of your work it is important to leave the wider conscious issues behind. You simply need to train your mind towards the discipline of writing. This is a discipline that benefits from regular practice and a regular routine in which this practice can be repeated. This approach is likely to allow you to feel you are making progress and, therefore, feel better about yourself as a writer.

I'm conscious writing these words that regular writing is a great notion, often hard to put into practice. Slotted in between wrestling children into bed, holding down a paid job, travelling here there and everywhere and/or arguing your own time on the one serviceable computer in a crowded house it seems like a luxury. In an ideal world there would be time to write and a recognition of its importance. If you live in such a world, you may only need the first suggestion for regular writing listed below. If not, I have some practical suggestions that do fit into limited time and space.

Regular practice of the craft will improve your abilities. You can set yourself targets at the earliest stage. The following exercises all share some things in common. They provide a purpose for writing designed to improve your abilities and focus your concentration. They depend on self-discipline and your own recognition that devoting regular time is essential if you are going to make a commitment to writing. Finally, they are in the pattern established in this chapter. Loose exercises which aim only to develop your skills and your ability to think. The only pressure on you is pressure to commit time and effort to produce the work.

Exercise 4

Adopt one of the following models as a regular writing activity. Activity 'i' is aimed at people who have no problems with regard to time and space to write. The other activities should suit the busiest of people. They have proven useful to students who claim to have no time to develop their writing. If this is your first regular writing activity it is advisable to concentrate on one of these exercises for a week or two before moving on to the more complex activities in the book. If you are already a regular writer you may still have something to gain from attempting one of these exercises as a means of liberating a creative stream of thoughts.

Writing exercises

i: Set yourself a regular time of between 30 minutes and 90 minutes each day to sit down and work on a piece of writing. Set about this with no clear intention of what you will produce. Simply start with a general notion that you will write a story, a collection of poems or fragments of work collecting your thoughts. The only things off limits are pieces of work aimed at a market, promoting a set opinion or deliberately aimed at some person(s) you know. Your target is simply to keep writing like this for a set period of time in an environment that will get you familiar with the essential thought processes and self-discipline.

ii: If time is a problem find one place in the day where you can, at least, get thinking time to yourself. Invent a fictitious character, a person with whom you want to talk and share. Find time every day to talk to this person in your mind. Start by telling them about yourself and how your life is going. After 3 or 4 days let them talk to you. In the short time you have to do this use a notepad. At the end of each mental conversation jot down any phrases of dialogue that struck you as inventive or informative. Also note down any interesting developments in the story of your character that come to light. When you have time, build these fragments into a longer piece of work exploring the relationship between you and your friend.

iii: Harness the pressures on you with a daily session of a few minutes writing fragments of prose. Start one piece of work headed *These Things Are True* and find a few minutes a day to write down something you know to be true. Concentrate on subjects that are part of your everyday life. Write short fragments about the people you meet, the things you do and your insights into the world. Each fragment should last between 100 and 200 words.

Consider the following examples:
Both of the following examples illustrate the value of being able to write and build on the basic knowledge you hold. One is a success story. One isn't.

A success: Recently I was talking to a writing student. A very young single parent struggling to keep studying, raise her child and make ends meet. I was delivering a class on building character into a radio script. This seemed too time-consuming for her in the 7-day turn-around time I'd allowed. We got talking about the possibilities of drawing on her busy life and shaping what she knew. Within a minute we were into a discussion about how to put nappies on babies. I pointed out something I'd learned. The instructions on nappy packaging tell you how to put nappies on a body. They fail to warn you that babies range from newly born, placid islands of calm to 18-month-old self-determining human torpedoes. Putting on a nappy is an act that requires a grasp of psychology, a perfect sense of timing and a belief in your ability to achieve the impossible. It is also the perfect subject for a *These Things Are True* fragment. Putting on a nappy is an act that helps to define character. My student didn't have vast amounts of time to research character. She did have her own baby to face when she went home. Within a few minutes we'd gone from discussing a tough problem of time management to realising that a little reflective thinking could be the basis of a solution.

Not A Success: Mark Kram's book *Ghosts Of Manila* presents stories of the boxers Muhammad Ali and Joe Frazier. It considers the influences that shaped their characters. Muhammad Ali's father Cassius "Cash" Clay is quoted. The author paints a vivid picture of Cash Clay who worked as a sign painter. Occasionally he undertook other work, like painting church murals.

Asked by his son why Jesus and the angels were always white Cash Clay replied, "We supposed not to know who we are, and the white man thinks he knows who he is, so he the only one can tell what Jesus is or isn't. So he thinks." Once Cash Clay saw Andy Warhol's famous paintings of Campbells Soup Cans. Mark Kram quotes his response, "Ain't them white folks got some scams, my, my."

Mark Kram goes on to paint a picture of Cash Clay that shows a creative person capable of latching on to a range of ideas. A man who re-invented himself continually. "Cash slipped into many shapes. If he was in a Hindu mood, he'd take a rug, stretch it out under a sign he was working on, kneel on it and begin to chant. As a Mexican he'd sport a sombrero and pretend he was taking a siesta." [7] Despite his clear creative talents Cash Clay is presented as a frustrated figure. The implication being that his son, Muhammad Ali, learned some of his famous lateral thinking and showmanship from his father. In terms of creative writing we have an example of a man who did things outlined in all three of the writing activities that preceded this section. Cash clearly devoted regular time to developing the kind of fictions outlined in activity 'i' and his ability to find fictitious characters within himself is also established. Finally, his observations on race politics linked to images of Jesus and the work of Andy Warhol would easily work themselves into *These Things Are True* fragments. Cash Clay wasn't a writer, but he obviously had the ability to think like one. In reality, most people can develop fictions, characters and reflective thoughts. Cash Clay simply provides a vivid example of how this might happen.

The ability to generate thoughts doesn't make you a writer. You start to make yourself a writer when the recognition of your latent talent is linked to a regular practice of the craft. Taking this step may be daunting. Remember that attempting to focus this talent into writing is a positive act. It is also an act that can provide unexpected benefits and insights. The commitment may be frightening but so are the consequences of ignoring the urge to be courageous.

2. Journeys And Migrations

"You don't lead by pointing and telling people some place to go. You lead by going to that place and making a case."

"I like being a famous writer. Problem is, every once in a while you have to write something."

Ken Kesey

The previous chapter was called Seeds. Its exercises were geared towards germination. Their purpose simply being to enhance your imagination. To put life into your thinking that could be directed into writing. These exercises can provide you with the raw material for writing. The next step is to focus this activity to some agreed purpose. Once this has been achieved you have the foundations on which you can build the most ambitious work. The ambitions are up to you. The exercises from this point onwards are designed to help you to cut and shape the raw material of observations, fragments and ideas.

Ken Kesey's comments opening this chapter provide a useful guide to cutting and shaping your work. Firstly, it is important to realise that the things you want to write can only be written by you. Others may touch on the subject, make more money or make more people laugh but they are not you. Your voice and ambitions are uniquely yours and your unique quality will only become apparent when you write. It is up to you to claim your own voice and territory as a writer.

This chapter deals with finding a focus and purpose as a writer. Only you can make the decisions that give a value to the advice and exercises that follow. Try them and consider the results, even if they don't appeal to you at first glance. Writing does not have to be about making money. It does not have to be about breaking new creative ground. In the opening to his book *Word Power*, first published in 1983, Julian Birkett noted: 'It no longer makes sense to think about the future of a piece of writing only in terms either of publication or of being left to rot in a drawer, as if there was nothing in between.' [1]

Those words written at the start of the 1980s were describing a growth in publishing that was dependent on the falling costs of production. Since then the widespread availability of information technology has completely changed the world in which writers are employed. Some of the changes are obvious, the growth of new forms like the e-book and websites and the wide availability of specialist work through Internet-based mail order. Some of the other changes are only obvious if you take a look over time.

My local Pizza Express has a downstairs area with a large amount of book shelving. One book on display is *The Writers Handbook 1990*, all 531 pages of it. Next to my computer as I write these words I have the 2002 edition of the same book, boasting 842 pages. The additions over the 12 years were mostly accounted for by an increasing number of small publishers, independent media companies and specialist outlets of all kinds. There are more courses than there were 12 years ago. The course I run started in 1999, and there have been more since then. The simple fact is that falling production costs have generated more work in areas that had no commercial value 20 years ago. Break-even point for the sales of a book may now be measured in a few hundred copies, a sales figure that would rate as grim to disastrous in the past.

The development of information technology has also changed the way people present and think about their work. In the mid 1990s the JenniCAM website was claimed as the most popular hit of all. The site was based on a web cam linked to a computer and placed in the apartment of Jennifer Ringley. [2] The vast majority of those who logged on saw only an empty apartment. Some were rewarded with shots of Jenny herself, mainly sleeping. Occasionally there were glimpses of her doing something like getting dressed, getting undressed or talking on the telephone. There was a serious point to the site. Ringley was a website designer. Her popular site made a case for the power of material on the Internet and the urgency for companies to employ website designers.

The development of forms including websites and fanzines have had another major impact on writing. By allowing almost any idea and angle on a subject into the public arena they have further diluted the notion that there is anything approaching an absolute critical standard. Talking in terms of absolute values, like good and bad, is always fraught with difficulty. A comparison of the following three extracts does give some insight into the changing situation.

Eibhlin Conroy was a young girl in Ireland when the historic flight of Alcock and Brown landed on the West Coast of the country on 16 June 1919, marking the first successful crossing of the Atlantic by air:

> They flew right over our house at Munga, where Colonel Fruen lived. My mum went out with a big sheet. They were hovering around the place and my mum went out and took a big white sheet... she was trying to tell them that there was a great meadow there where they were hovering and to come down there. They were confused. I don't think they really knew where they were. [3]

Sylvia Smith has held a succession of temporary jobs. She has never married or had any children. This extract describes an event in her life in 1979:

1979 SAM

Sam was a fifty-five-year-old sales rep. We were both employees of the same clothing company. I was thirty-four and a private secretary to the managing director.

As I entered the showroom I heard Sam talking to the sales director. He was explaining why he'd been late for an appointment with a client the previous evening. He said "I broke down in my car last night." I interrupted and asked, "Didn't you have a hankie?" which brought some humour to the situation. [4]

Maya Angelou has worked as a poet, dancer, academic, film-maker and political activist. The following extract concludes an essay in the collection of essays, *Even The Stars Look Lonesome*:

Many people are graduated from teacher-training academies, but one has to have a calling to become a true teacher. And above all things, one needs a bounty of courage.

The calling informs the teacher that her knowledge is needed in new uncharted areas, and the courage makes the teacher dare the journey. My mother had both. [5]

These are short extracts, chosen to make a specific point. Taken, to a certain degree, out of context. However, it is worth considering what they show about changing patterns of writing. Maya Angelou is easily the most critically respected writer in evidence here. However, her comment in this extract is not one that relies on a phenomenal grasp of literature. It is based on pragmatic life experience. The kind of experience that often underpins collections of writing and observations from local writers groups. In the extracts above the story of the landing of Alcock and Brown is gathered from *Hidden Conamara*, a vivid and moving collection from a local writers group on the West Coast of Ireland. Eibhlin Conroy's short recollection recounts an event of importance to world history. Despite this, the very personal nature of the memory and the recording of the information in her own voice give it an authenticity that a more experienced writer would struggle to capture.

Agents and editors searching for best-selling work amongst new writers value writing that recounts monumental or unique events. Eibhlin Conroy's work is the only extract above that approaches this quality. However, the one surprise best-seller and high-profile work in this sequence is Sylvia Smith's *Misadventures*. The author was rejected by one agent on the grounds that she couldn't write to any standard suitable for publication. In *Misadventures*, her autobiography, she frankly admits that she is unsure of whether the work is worthy of publication. The book survived some rejections to find a home at Canongate, a respected publisher based in Edinburgh and best known for very individual authors likely to gain a critical following. The fragment featuring Sam makes up an entire chapter of the book. The book gathered a mixed reaction, one reviewer describing it admiringly as 'The most boring thing I have ever read,' whilst others believed it to be an elaborate hoax by a name writer. [6] It is a very strange autobiography. Full of incidental details and told in short scenes that proceed at an almost random pace. Stranger still is the fact that a number of major points are only mentioned in passing. The writer admits to many relationships with men by her mid-twenties, revealing they were all platonic to this point. No explicit details of her love life are ever revealed. She also alludes to other events including a car crash and a row with her parents so severe as to lead her to leave home. There are no direct accounts of these events. *Misadventures* became one of the most talked about new works of 2001.

These fragments of work demonstrate the way that the previous certainties in the world of writing are steadily eroding. This leaves those teaching writing with less absolute truth to impart. Historically, books on the teaching of writing have been full of earnest advice on narrative structure, characterisation and details of what editors are looking for. Most of this advice still has a use and some of it is included in this book. However, the examples above help to demonstrate that there is now an outlet for almost any kind of writing. If all else fails, self-published pamphlets and the Internet offer publication at a rock bottom price. These forms of publication are still getting cheaper and the future is likely to offer even more possibilities for writers to place their work. New media and cheaper publication in the traditional forms make it more likely that a writer will find some form of publication. There are two major drawbacks in this situation. Firstly, it remains as hard as ever to achieve high-profile success. Secondly, getting any kind of point across still demands that you perform as a writer. You must have a clarity of purpose, skilful delivery and the willingness to put in some hard work. Ken Kesey's quotes are both succinct and accurate. You'll make your points when your writing goes to a place and obliges your readers to follow. And, you have to accept that there is always a time when you simply have to shut up and put up.

So, if you want to be published that badly, there is a good chance you'll succeed in some form. The rest of the chapter will concentrate on general exercises to help you find a purpose for your work and build on the basic skills already established.

The writer Paul Magrs teaches on the University Of East Anglia's Creative Writing programme. In a book on creative writing drawn from the experiences of the teaching staff he noted, 'The things a writer publishes are just postcards; extended cards sent back from the distance they've reached.' [7] A useful focus with which to start the exercises that end this chapter.

If we are to make the information-gathering exercises of the previous chapter count we must consider methods of building these into focused work. I have already said that this book is not a primer on the use of the English language. However, it is important that we briefly consider the use of language as we work towards exercises on complete works of writing. It is also vital that we complete an exercise in focusing thoughts and ideas into a specific form. One detailed exercise in each area is included here along with suggestions for further journeys and migrations from the observation and recording covered in the previous chapter.

What You Say

This is a book about creativity and craft. Not a work dedicated to spelling, grammar and punctuation. In due course there will be suggestions about further reading and study to ensure that the basics of English usage are covered. Language usage is one element of the armoury Stephen King refers to as a writer's "tool kit."

The following outline and exercise provides an insight into the kind of work you can undertake to help you identify your skills as a writer and put your ideas into their most effective form. They concern the use and structure of sentences. When you master sentence structure, you are well equipped to tackle complete works of all kinds.

Sentences are the main organisational tool in English. They indicate meanings, relative importance, time and specific details. Words are a sign system. As writers, we need sentences to create meaning. There are a few basic rules about sentences.

Complete sentences contain a verb and subject. A verb is, literally, a word indicating an action, state or occurrence. The subject is the person or thing attached to the main verb. For example, the shortest sentence in *The Bible* is 'Jesus wept.' The verb 'wept' is an action, 'Jesus' is the subject.

Some sentences contain more than one verb. When this occurs there is generally a main verb. This is the major verb, carrying the important information. In these more complex sentences there are still clear links between verb and subject. Such linked sections containing a verb and subject are called clauses. You might arrive home to find the following note waiting for you:

I've gone to sorting office to get a parcel. See you about 6.00.

It's the kind of message people leave for each other every day. It is also a good example of building clauses into direct and meaningful English. The opening sentence has two verbs 'gone' and 'get.' In this opening sentence 'gone' is the main verb because it carries the major part of the information, explaining the absence of the writer. 'gone to sorting office' is one clause, 'get a parcel' is another.

Some verbs are followed by a complement. This is not a subject or object but a word used to describe some part of the subject's existence. Verbs like 'are' and 'appears,' which are linked to some state of existence, are good examples of complements. An example is:

They (subject) are (verb) uneasy (complement).

We are looking at the cold constituents of language and writing. But understanding the most basic of sentence rules is central to effective writing. Used skilfully, an understanding of these rules creates work that outlives the writer. The following extract opens Mark Twain's classic *The Adventures Of Tom Sawyer*. Look at the subtleties of character Twain manages to build into the first complete paragraph which describes Tom's Aunt Polly.

"Tom!"

No answer.

"Tom!"

No answer.

"What's gone with that boy, I wonder? You Tom!"

The old lady pulled her spectacles down and looked over them, about the room; then she put them up and looked out under them. She seldom or never looked through them for so small a thing as a boy, for they were her state pair, the pride of her heart, and were built for 'style' not service; she could have seen through a pair of stove lids as well. She looked perplexed a

41

moment and said, not fiercely, but still loud enough for the furniture to hear, "Well, I lay if I get hold of you I'll -"

Originally published in 1876, the book is written in a complex style unsuited to the punchier prose styles of this century. The characters and values in the story have also dated. Despite this, the description of Aunt Polly built on the brilliant observations of subject and object still work effectively. The pride and sense of self-worth in Aunt Polly are demonstrated in her adjustments of her spectacles and the acute observation of the loudness she brings to her final sentence of speech. A superb use of a complement appears in a clause about her spectacles.

They (subject) were (verb) her state pair (complement).

In other words these were spectacles that said everything about her status and position. Their practical use was a secondary consideration.

Writers practising sentence use is the equivalent of musicians practising riffs or arpeggios. Not producing complete works, but still making space for creativity and honing vital skills. Good sentence writing depends on skilful choice of verbs, confidence concerning the use of main and subordinate verbs and the deft placement of information around subject and main verb. It is also important to give yourself the space to be creative.

Exercise 5

Complete the following exercises on writing sentences:

i. Gather a selection of 10 photographs which show some action. Include some of your own, for example family pictures. Include a few news photographs and some others from dramatised events, for example pictures taken from a TV listings magazine. Describe the main events of each photograph in a single sentence giving each sentence careful thought in terms of main verb, any subordinate verbs, subject and complement.

ii. Carry out the exercise above in a limited way, repeating the same formula but assuming an audience of children under 10 for your sentences. You will have to aim for simplicity with all elements of your sentences.

iii. Gather the notes you made in exercise 3. Use them as raw material for a short story of between 400 and 600 words. Build the information carefully into sentences that add a lot of description to the story.

iv. Complete a 400 word 'word mime.' This is a short description of someone in which you convey as much information as possible through descriptions of their movements and surroundings. You are not allowed to use speech or biographical information. You will complete the exercise most effectively if you are skilful with the use of verbs, especially in relation to main and subordinate verb use.

v. Take two clean sheets of paper. Write down 50 verbs on one sheet and fifty possible subjects on the other. The subjects can be as varied as 'The Dog,' 'Adolf Hitler' and/or 'My lover.' Combine one verb and one subject to create a series of twenty independent nonsensical sentences. These should observe the rules of sentence structure. The aim is to produce vivid images which show the creative possibilities of an individual sentence. Consider the example below.

Graham Rawle has written the popular series of *Lost Consonants*. In this series, produced in newspapers, postcards and books, Rawle presents cut-and-paste pictures compiled from very unlikely elements. Each image is supported by a single sentence describing what we see. The running joke is that somewhere in the sentence there is one missing consonant, (i.e., one missing letter which is not a vowel). One picture shows a Labrador dog standing upright in a kitchen, wearing oven gloves, looking over its shoulder and holding a tray of fresh jam tarts. The caption reads 'Every time the doorbell rang, the dog started baking.' [8]

What You See

Focusing ideas into images is a skill central to all writing. It is a vital component in areas that rely on vision, like cartoons and television. It is also vital in areas that rely on the audience conjuring up their own images, like novels and radio scripts.

One form perfect for building the skill is the composition of haiku poetry. In the traditional Japanese form, shown earlier in the writing of Basho, there are typically three elements. The presentation of a situation, in the form of an image is the first part of the haiku. A sudden perception or insight related to the image forms the final part. In between is a 'kireji.' Literally, a break. Haiku written in English typically use strong punctuation, like a full stop or exclamation mark, as a kireji. Haiku are typically written in 17 syllables along a pattern of 5-7-5. A break, in the form of punctuation doesn't count in the syllables. Often the first part of the haiku takes the opening twelve syllables. Haiku are most effective in recording scenes and perceptions. They tend to lose impact when the writer attempts to impose him/herself into the scene. I wrote the following haiku to demonstrate the form in English.

> Clean plastic tables
> Of burger cafe at night.
> Bright moon reflecting

The haiku records something I saw. It also shows how the form is perfect to add a quality to an image. In this case the sudden perception that the tables in my local McDonald's provided a perfect reflecting surface for a full moon at midnight. The intention of the two parts of the haiku is to oppose the image of the man-made shining objects, the tables, with the brilliant and eternal shining of the moon. This is a quality partly conveyed in the two descriptions of the 'clean' plastic tables and the 'bright' moon. 'Bright' is a word with more positive connotations and 'clean' is a word that implies simply a state. The suggestion is that the tables were only clean because someone had taken the trouble to clean them.

Haiku make a perfect training ground for aspiring writers because they allow us to focus an essential skill and something we do all the time - reading meaning into things we see. As writers we generally have an innate sense of the feeling and point behind the images we create. It is possible in these situations to become so involved in what we think we are saying that we lose sight of the need to use words with skill and precision. In a 17-syllable haiku skill and precision are vital.

Exercise 6

Create a haiku to record the following:

i. A news photograph in the next paper you see. You should concentrate on a photograph of an event, not a celebrity or posed picture. In creating your final five syllables try to capture the quality the photographer was attempting to portray.

ii. A family photograph evoking a particularly strong emotion to you because it captures an important quality in a person. For example, a picture of a child that captures a trusting and helpless quality.

44

iii. The next surprising thing you see that makes an impression on you.

iv. Capture the essence of one of the fragments entitled *These Things Are True*, created for exercise 4, in a haiku.

3. Me, Myself And I

'The point is not what we can actually do. What counts here is
what people think we can do: almost EVERYTHING.'

Bert Keizer, *Dancing With Mr D.*

We've looked at the basics and made some decisions. The exercises so
far provide vital skills. From this point, the combination of skills and your
decisions is the basis of your making meaning, making money or making a
mess. The decisions are yours. The remaining subjects are vast. Each
remaining chapter provides an insight, a series of examples and some consideration of how you might employ the information in making significant
decisions. The chapters outline possibilities and show you the implications
of decisions. That is all anyone setting out to explain writing can usefully
hope to do. Any more intervention than this and the writing you produce is
not really your writing at all. This chapter takes a detailed look at your position as a writer. It concentrates mainly on extracts, from books. The points
made apply to all kinds of writing.

Point Of View

A point of view is literally the position from which you choose to present
your material. Understanding the potential for meaning and exploration
offered from this position can take a lifetime. Frequently, the first notice-
able thing about a writer is the position he or she chooses to adopt with
regard to their work. The best writers can explore a subject from a range of
viewpoints. The poet Simon Armitage produced the book *All Points North*
in such a way. Starting at a grim side-on portrait of the elderly couple in a
cafe on the cover, the book is an exploration of the very quality of Northern-
ness. At various points Armitage samples news stories, presents a fictional
story and reports things he knows to be true. In the latter case these events
are from his own life and those of others. In doing so he changes point of
view, talks in the first, second and third person and lets the whole cacoph-
ony of images and ideas deliver *All Points North*.

The book opens with the following tale:

> True story. Last winter, three men from a village in West York-
> shire went fishing off the coast near Scarboro, and hauled in an
> unexploded mine from the Second World War. A crowd gath-
> ered to look at the bomb, and a reporter from local television

46

turned up to interview the men on the beach. When the reporter
asked one of them if they'd been frightened, he said, "No, we're
alright, us." [1]

It's a perfectly selected story to open an exploration of people and place.
In the opening section Armitage's own memories also inform his understanding of the link between the North and its people. The opening section
is called 'Where You're At.' In reality, it is a history of the writer and his
perceptions of the place. He addresses us in the second person. But this is
not what it seems because the references to 'You' and 'Your' are simply a
way of saying that we, as readers, are him. In other words the first person 'I'
and 'me' is indistinguishable from the second person.

Your front door opens out on to some of the most empty and
dangerous countryside in Britain. Hundreds of square miles of
saturated earth and rotting peat, a kind of spongy version of the
sea. When you were a kid you walked across the moors looking
for dead bodies, but found tractor tyres instead, or fridge-freez-
ers, or crash helmets, miles from anything or anywhere. The
only other thing to do was to break into air shafts above the railway tunnel and drop stones on the Liverpool train. [2]

The book goes on to present the place and author in a variety of guises.
Sometimes simply letting collisions of images identify the North:

...where Jarvis Cocker meets Geoffrey Boycott, where Emily
Bronte meets David Batty, where Ted Hughes meets Darren
Gough, where David Hockney meets Peter Sutcliffe, where
Brian Glover meets Henry Moore, and where Bernard Ingham
meets Prince Naseem Hamed, or at least if there's any justice he
does. [3]

Simon Armitage's book goes on to explore the subject from several other
perspectives. A fictional story, *Jerusalem*, presents intransigent and hardened northern values in a grimly comic tale. The same grim humour that
underpins two phone conversations in which Direct Line ring the poet and
enquire after his change of profession from probation officer to poet. They
explain the need to up his premium by £82 because he now falls under their
Entertainment and Leisure classification making him, apparently, more at
risk from "nutters and all that."
I start my Professional Writing students on reading extracts from *All
Points North* because it shows clearly the way that differing points of view
can be used to present a subject. You can find a focus in your own experi-

47

ence and imagination. You can gather scraps of stories or move your viewpoint to make some small action into a metaphor for a greater truth. All help to tell stories and present your own unique vision.

In his book *Writing In Action* [4] the writer and lecturer Paul Mills presents four perspectives in terms of autobiographical viewpoint: portrait, narrative, poetic/imaginative and change of thinking. Portrait writing uses images and details to present a reality. It relies on a reader decoding the picture in words very much as if it was a picture on a gallery wall or a photograph in a magazine. Narrative autobiography is the form most often used in popular autobiographical writing. Narrative writing uses the classic elements of storytelling. Poetic/imaginative writing makes connections which are far from obvious but which may be used to illuminate a story, bringing additional meanings. In autobiography any aspect of an autobiographical story can be presented in an unusual way. The difference between this and poetic/imaginative is the way that change of thinking can move right away from direct autobiography and simply use details and observations to move a reader or audience towards a particular understanding. In many cases autobiographical writing uses more than one of these viewpoints. However, most writers work mainly from one viewpoint and draw on others when they need to add effects or information.

Consider the following examples. All concern death and each relies mainly on one different point of view from Mills' list.

Portrait: One writer described Sherwin B Nuland's point of view on death as 'brutal, unmetahphorical fact,' going on to point out that Nuland gave us death 'in its biological and clinical reality.' [5] Nuland is a surgeon with over three decades of clinical experience. His book *How We Die* is divided into chapters dealing with varied causes of death that open with self-explanatory titles like 'The Strangled Heart,' 'The Doors To Death Of The Aged' and 'Murder And Serenity.' [6]

Considering the first patient to die in front of him Nuland admits to fear and an emotional reaction to death. But, it is an element of himself that remains in check throughout his book. Few deaths are more emotionally fraught on the living than the suicide of young people. Nuland considers the most common methods employed, keeping an objective distance whilst pitching facts and images into a portrait.

> The by-now-well-known technique of swallowing a quantity of sleeping pills just before enclosing one's head in a firmly secured airtight plastic bag does work quite well... .Because the bag is so small, the oxygen is used up quickly, well before the rebreathed carbon dioxide has any significant effect. Rapid cere-

bral failure ensues, but what really causes death is that a low blood-oxygen level slows the heart quickly to a complete standstill and the arrest of circulation. There may be some symptoms of acute heart failure as the rate of ventricular contraction decreases, but it hardly makes any difference, because dying is so efficiently accomplished. Although one would assume there might be terminal convulsions or vomiting inside the bag, this apparently rarely, if ever, occurs. Dr. Wayne Carver, the chief medical examiner of the state of Connecticut has seen enough of such suicides to assure me that their faces are neither blue nor swollen. They look, in fact, quite ordinary - just dead.

Nuland taught Medicine at Yale University when he wrote *How We Die*. It is autobiographical because he uses his experience and appears in the middle of the objective descriptions. In the above extract Dr Wayne Carver assures the author, making it clear that we are reading the collected wisdom of the author, not simply a list of facts. The point of view is deliberately selected by Nuland. He sought the information on this form of suicide and had choices about presenting it. Nuland's perspective may be unremitting and harsh. In teaching medicine and surviving a lengthy and successful career in the field, it may also be a means of survival. Writing in this style retains a power because the viewpoint is so clearly defined. We have a close-up view of hard factual details that would otherwise be kept from us. Portrait and factual styles are often at their best in such situations. The continued popularity of, for example, true crime writing is very much down to detailed descriptions of crimes like murders. These passages outline sounds like screams, desperate struggles and spare few details on the messy outcome of successful attempts to kill.

Narrative: Thomas Lynch is an undertaker and acclaimed poet. He has also produced two books of meditative essays. *The Undertaking* and *Bodies In Motion And At Rest*. In the opening essay in *The Undertaking*, subtitled *Life Studies From The Dismal Trade*, Lynch talks about his work.

> Every year I bury a couple hundred of my townspeople. Another two or three dozen I take to the crematory to be burned. I sell caskets, burial vaults and urns for the ashes. I have a sideline in headstones and monuments. I do flowers on commission. [7]

It is a portrait start as the author sets the scene. He continues with a statistical breakdown of the size of the local population, the predictable rates and causes of death and a rough outline of how he makes a living. However, by this point he is working his statistics into a story.

> Imagine a large room into which you coax one thousand people. You slam the doors in January, leaving them plenty of food and drink, colour TVs, magazines and condoms... ..Now for the magic part - come late December when you throw open the doors, only 991.6, give or take, will shuffle out upright.

By this point Lynch's viewpoint is that of a storyteller, injecting his personality and perspective into the situation. The watershed in this regard comes with a refrain that runs through his opening essay.

> The dead don't care.

It's a statement that allows the author to explain the key point. He deals with the dead but works for the living. He illustrates this truth with a narrative.

> Last Monday morning Milo Hornsby died. Mrs Hornsby called at two a.m. to say that Milo had *expired* and would I take care of it.

Lynch goes out in the middle of the night to deal with the situation but is clear about what he is doing.

> I do not haul to my senses... for Milo's sake. Milo doesn't have any sake any more. I go for her...

The author goes on to detail events in his earlier life when Milo, the owner of a laundry, helped him. When Lynch's first wife left him with their children and a business to run Milo's van picked up their laundry and kept them in clean clothes and bedding until Lynch employed a housekeeper. Settling the bill he was charged sixty dollars for the washing. He asked about the charges for pick-up and delivery "for stack and folding and sorting by size, for saving my life and the lives of our children." Milo tells him there is no charge. Explaining that "One hand washes the other."

The essay closes with Lynch examining death itself in a narrative sense. The dead Milo is presented in terms of his absence in an ongoing story.

> What we buried... had ceased to be Milo. Milo had become the idea of himself... his widow's loss of appetite and trouble sleeping.

The narrative approach used here allows the author to show compassion and bring the reader into the story. Lynch makes serious points about life and death using drama. The examples in his stories give us scope for reflection. It is the approach most commonly used in best-selling biographical writing. This is easily the most accessible autobiographical style because it closely resembles the most popular writing of all, fiction. It also corresponds closely to the way that the majority of readers think. We generally see ourselves within some kind of narrative, even if we are only imagining the things that are likely to happen to us in the next hour or day.

Poetic/imaginative: Bert Keizer's book *Dancing With Mr D.* [8] is a meditative memoir based on the experiences of a Dutch physician working with the terminally ill in a country sometimes allowing suicide. It presents fragments, each considering some aspect of Keizer's work and the issue of life and death. *Dancing With Mr D.* presents death as a confusing and frustrating conundrum. This work questions who doctors are working for, showing Keizer helping the living and dying at each other's expense at different times. It is ultimately a book about limitations. Limitations of life, the limited abilities of doctors to cure and limited understanding between people. It is, therefore, fitting that the short passages that are compiled into the whole work should focus and explore rather than present any overall explanation. Each fragment has the same quality of focus we see in poetry. Poetic devices, like metaphor and simile [9], are frequently employed.

Keizer also dramatises some issues. One vivid exploration of the powerlessness experienced by doctors is presented in a short dialogue.

- "Doctor, why am I ill?"

- "valve leaks."

- "yes, but why me?"

- "wait, I'll get the vicar."

In a later fragment, titled 'Cancer Research And Rainmaking,' the author uses the crude science of creating rain to give the reader an insight into the grim realities of progress in cancer research.

"Ah, well, yes, but you see, the point is not what we can actually do. What counts here is what people think we can do: almost EVERYTHING. At this moment you'd find it hard to beat our PR. This belief in our virtual omnipotence doesn't need to be backed up by facts. Everybody loves to believe it. The other day I heard again on the evening news that there's been considerable progress again in cancer research. This is, I assure you, the absolute crap that you hear every few months. Cancer research has been on the brink of a major breakthrough for the last thirty or forty years and the funny thing is that everybody believes this without anything ever breaking through."

"I can't believe that's the truth."

"See what I mean? You fall into it too, and you couldn't tell cancer research from rain-making."

The conversation goes on with Keizer pointing out that reports claiming a breakthrough and that 50 per cent of cancers can be cured are missing a vital point. According to Keizer the figures have not significantly improved in the best part of half a century. It is simply that the PR spin on the information suggests that each new breakthrough is a magnificent achievement.

The use of the comparison with rainmaking hangs there unexplained, inviting us to consider it further. The point Keizer is making concerns the way we perceive cancer research advancing like some methodical certainty. He doesn't labour the rainmaking comparison although it is, to all intents and purposes, presented as a simile. Rainmaking is a crude science that proceeds on the back of vague ideas and some basis in fact.

Dispensing death drugs, Keizer belongs to a select few physicians. His unusual circumstances and the perspective it gives him on life are effectively represented with poetic devices like metaphor and simile. Although the book is an autobiography, the poetic technique is more effective than narrative in this situation because Keizer's most telling points are those that separate his experience from the rest of us and the use of poetic devices forces our thinking into points of view that emphasise this distance.

Other writers have used the same approach. In December 2001 BBC Radio 4 started the innovative, *Signs Of Life*, in which drama was intercut with documentary recordings to give an insight into terminal conditions. In the first programme the account of a father who had lost his children to Cystic Fibrosis was worked around a drama in which a man was telling his story of being the only survivor of a sunken ship. The metaphor of drowning was central to the programme. A metaphor in that the overwhelming tragedy of terminal illness threatens to overwhelm us and also a literal comparison in that Cystic Fibrosis is a disease that attacks the lungs, literally drowning the sufferer.

Change Of Thinking: The following extracts, taken from the script of the movie *Monty Python's The Meaning Of Life*, are not an obvious autobiography. They have an autobiographical basis and their inventiveness makes them a highly suitable basis from which to explain the change of thinking point of view. In change of thinking autobiography the writer generally represents changes in their thinking through the development of images and ideas that lead the reader through similar changes.

I'd like to take this change a little further than Paul Mills. It seems to me that change of thinking as an approach can usefully be employed to totally change a reality whilst still drawing from autobiography. This is a natural extension from the poetic devices of *Dancing With Mr D*. Monty Python's movie script, and especially the scenes on death, appear to me to be a perfect example. [10]

The movie runs, literally, from birth to death and finally life after death. The death sequence opens with an animation in which a tree stands resplendent with autumn leaves in front of an aged family vault in a cemetery.

> DISTRAUGHT MALE VOICE: I just can't go on. I'm no good anymore, goodbye... goodbye... aaaargh!... Aaargh!
>
> *A LEAF FALLS TO THE GROUND*
>
> DISTRAUGHT FEMALE VOICE: Oh my God! What'll I do!? I can't live without him... I... aaaargh!
>
> *ANOTHER LEAF FALLS*
>
> DISTRAUGHT CHILDREN'S VOICES: Mummy... Mummy... Mummy... Daddy
>
> *TWO MORE LEAVES FALL*
>
> MORE DISTRAUGHT VOICES: Oh no! Aaaargh!
>
> *ALL THE REMAINING LEAVES FALL WITH ONE ACCORD.*

In a scene which follows shortly afterwards, The Grim Reaper visits an isolated house. He taps on the door with his scythe, a middle-class couple appear. Geoffrey, the husband, suggests the call is inconvenient as they have people over for dinner. Angela, his wife, invites "Mr Death" inside.

We meet the other guests, including an American couple. Death keeps on insisting, "I am Death," despite their patronising attitude. Angela has already told her guests that he is a man from the village who has "Come about the reaping."

A bizarre conversation ensues as Death attempts to convince everyone they are dead. They try to draw him into conversation. Eventually Death makes his point.

> GRIM REAPER: I am not of this world.

He backs up the statement by walking into the middle of the table.
An American guest, Mr Katzenberg, still can't take it in.

MR KATZENBERG: Just one moment, I would like to express on behalf of everyone here what a really unique experience this is.

The group understand on one level but still insist on debating the whole issue. Mr Katzenberg listens then wades in with his next assertion.

MR KATZENBERG: Let me tell you what I think we're dealing with here, a potentially positive learning experience.

GRIM REAPER: Shut up! Shut up you American. You always talk, you Americans, you talk and you say 'Let me tell you something' and 'I just wanna say this.' Well you're dead now, so shut up.

The point finally hits home. The stunned group still argue. They can't understand how they all died together until, with a lingering shot in the film, The Grim Reaper's skeletal hand points slowly downward into the smoked salmon mousse. The embarrassed hostess splutters her apologies.

ANGELA: Honestly, darling, I'm so embarrassed... I mean to serve salmon with botulism at a dinner party is social death.

At which point the group proceed to the afterlife.

Python's strengths as a comedy team included their intelligence. Formed from the cream of the comedy talent at the universities of Oxford and Cambridge, they were amongst the best-educated minds of their generation. Their best work often involved applying this intelligence to a well-established subject in a way that dismantled myths and beliefs. This approach was the basis of the group's movies. *Monty Python And The Holy Grail* presented King Arthur as a misunderstood character. In one scene, two peasants manage to work out that Arthur is a king simply because he isn't covered in shit. In the celebrated and controversial *Life Of Brian* a completely average man, Brian, gathers a following who see him as a messiah simply because they are desperate to believe. They interpret his mundane actions as miraculous. Brian's mother is forced to address the mob at one point:

"He isn't the messiah, he's a very naughty boy."

Change of thinking was always likely to be a strength of a group brought together in an academic environment. The Pythons had been rewarded with academic marks for the skills that would eventually underpin their comedy careers. The change of thinking strategy in writing is obvious in the notion that leaves don't fall naturally, they commit suicide. Similarly the dinner party presents two kinds of death. The guests are poisoned but the hostess dies twice, the second time when she admits that her actions represent social death.

The Meaning Of Life isn't an obvious autobiography but it does include autobiographical elements. It borrows heavily from a background in which the writers examined academic issues from a range of angles and it presents an acute observation of a section of society who give dinner parties and debate a range of issues. In this instance, they struggle to actually understand anything, even the most fundamental human truth, their own mortality.

This chapter set out to explore point of view. The examples presented have examined a fundamental human issue from four viewpoints. Establishing point of view effectively and being clear about both your decision and the implication of such a decision are central to achieving your aims as a writer. Point of view is also a necessary element in making meaning, making money and cutting and shaping plots.

The chapter opened with a quote from Bert Keizer.

> The point is not what we can actually do. What counts here is what people think we can do: almost EVERYTHING.

You know now that this is a sentence uttered by Keizer himself within the section on 'Cancer Research And Rainmaking.' However, I think it is also useful to employ a change of thinking approach yourself at this point. Keizer was making the point that people come to doctors expecting anything to be possible. They need to believe this. Audiences frequently approach writing with the same expectations. The wildly varying treatments of death that have made up the bulk of this chapter show you the range of escapism, insight and invention that can be brought to one subject by four pieces of work.

Unlike doctors, writers can do almost everything. Our only concern in this regard is how long we can sustain the belief of an audience in our work. In the few minutes it takes to watch Michael Jackson's video for 'Earth Song,' the reversal of global ecological damage, including the revival of a dead elephant, makes complete sense. As much sense as a game of Quiddich, the genuine existence of a Polar Bear on top of a Fox's Glacier Mint or Desperate Dan's demolition of an entire cow in a pie. In a less health conscious era Dan also smoked. Cigarettes were out of the question. Dan's smoking habits involved igniting a dustbin full of rubbish and inhaling the resulting fumes through a length of drainpipe. The things outlined in this paragraph are all examples of creative ideas. None of them literally possible, all of them the result of thinking that was written into scripts and brought into being successfully. Audiences in every case responded positively.

What matters is what people think we can do. We can learn the skills and set out to employ them in the pursuit of audiences, employment and the creation of meaning. But, in the end, we'll make our own luck.

So far the exercises have required you to build skills and attempt small, fragmentary pieces of work. These are a good start. Now it's time to complete a more ambitious piece of writing and consider the effect of point of view.

Exercise 7

Take one of the following titles:

The Final Curtain
Life, The Universe And Everything
My Brilliant Career
Cloud Nine

All of these titles have appeared somewhere in a highly successful piece of creative work and all are broadly suggestive of some wider issue. Make one title yours by developing a piece of work with a strongly established point of view. Complete one of the following:

i: A short story of between 1000 and 1500 words.

ii: A script for a short radio drama running to around ten minutes. [Radio drama scripts average 40 seconds per page of script]

In the case of the radio drama, do not worry unduly about how a script should be set out. The purpose of the exercise is to arrange the idea so the point of view is clearly expressed. What matters is that the speeches, sound effects and other items are planned logically and completed to your satisfaction.

Before writing your work, make notes and keep on referring to them. Make a firm decision on which point of view to adopt and how to sustain your point of view throughout the work. If adopting a poetic/imaginative or change of thinking point of view you will need careful planning. Using something as a poetic device or changing the nature of a subject is a highly creative approach but also fraught with difficulty. However, consider that, amongst the examples above the most successful work in financial terms is the extract from the Monty Python movie.

4. People, Places And Plots

'Dignity is an affectation, cute but eccentric, like learning French or collecting scarves. And it's fleeting and incredibly mercurial. And subjective. So fuck it.'

Dave Eggers, *A Heartbreaking Work Of Staggering Genius*

"We are all of us in the gutter. But some of us are looking at the stars."

Oscar Wilde

Point of view is simply one of the limits we need to establish to create writing that achieves its aims. The next chapter involves coming down from an overall viewpoint and getting to grips with the issues that will shape the insides of a piece of work. My apologies to anyone who finds Dave Eggers' outburst at the start of the chapter offensive. I think it warranted because it succinctly states a point that applies to all writing. Dignity, in the form of the illusion that we create work as if by some divine, and effortless right, is an affectation. It is the creation of press offices in publishing houses and movie studios. Put simply, it is the creation of people who stand to benefit if they can convince the public that they are selling a work of genius. Very little work is created this easily and almost none of the work created easily achieves high sales or high impact.

So now it's time to tackle the items that give work shape, meaning, sales value and integrity. These issues - tough decisions about events, characters and the progress of a piece of work - are the most common source of pain and frustration for writers. You may have worried and fretted your way through earlier exercises and examples but this chapter is all about the 99% of writing that is the result of perspiration. We need to investigate and understand the key elements that help to construct a piece of writing.

Plot

Put simply a plot is a series of events that take place within a narrative sequence. The things that make up the story. As the writer you have overall control of the sequence of events, the way that we move from time to time and place to place. Non-fiction items, like documentaries and articles, are also planned along plot lines. In such cases the work may explore issues by telling stories. It may, also, simply present facts. Non-fiction work still depends on structure, sequence, character and the way that ideas are represented.

Depending on your intentions as a writer you may be obliged to treat plot, place and character in a particular way. For example, some markets are so dependent on formula writing that they will send you, on request, outlines of how to cut and shape your work. The BBC use freelance writers to provide material for their radio comedy programmes. Shows like *The News Huddlines* credit a huge company of writers every week. The BBC produce detailed writers guidelines for comedy and drama writers. These define structure, running times and other issues. Whatever your ideas about people, places and plots your only chance of BBC acceptance with a new drama for television or radio involves paying attention to their guidelines. For example:

> A series creates characters and uses them to tell a self-contained story each week. It can potentially run indefinitely, Examples *Ballykissangel*, *Casualty*, *Silent Witness*.

The guidelines go on to specify key issues. Aspiring writers should, for example, include:

> A detailed character breakdown explaining each protagonist's past, how they behave, what it is about them that will motivate the action of the series, how they are likely to respond to situations etc. [1]

There are other guidelines produced by other companies. Romantic publishers Mills and Boon and DC Thompson of Dundee, famous for teenage photo story magazines and women's publications as well as *Beano* and *Dandy*, will also send out guidelines for aspiring freelancers. So will card companies like Emotional Rescue. One thing almost all of these documents share in common is their clear sense of purpose and their emphasis on focus for the writer.

Whatever your intention, those likely to receive your work would give you similar advice. Plan it carefully, execute it to perfection and have a clear idea of character and situation.

Plot Planning

Depending on your intended writing, plot may be an absolute necessity or a useful area of speculation. If you were to reply to an advert for a writing course in the national press it is likely that you would find yourself being taught some basic plot-planning technique. Such courses teach a specific brand of professional writing, encouraging their writers in the first instance to prepare work for the kind of magazines that take unsolicited short fiction and non-fiction filler. Short unsolicited fiction for magazines is generally written to very tight word limits and limitations of style. In such cases a plot plan is vital.

An experienced writer might dispense with a plan but this is because, as Basho suggested, he or she will know all the rules and have forgotten them. In other words, the discipline of commercial fiction will be second nature to such a writer. Plot plans vary but the following is an example of the way such a plan might be outlined for a 1000-1500 word story.

Scene 1

Situation
Conflict/test
Key character's major active trait
Result

Scene 2

Situation
Conflict/test
Key character's major active trait
Result

Scene 3

Situation
Conflict/test
Black moment
Key character's major active trait
Result

A novel written to a formula, like a Mills and Boon title, might employ a plot plan based on the same elements but stretched to include more complex plot items and cover a narrative over 50-55,000 words. The plot plan encourages writers to focus each scene around a well-planned event. The conflict/test is also part of the plan. Mass market fiction of all kinds often revolves around placing tests in the way of a character with whom the audience can sympathise. Each test keeps the reader, viewer or listener closely involved with the character. It is also vital that the character does something active in response to the test. In hugely ambitious and expensive productions, like James Bond movies, this active response might be truly spectacular. In less spectacular work, like television soap operas, the active responses might be simple movements like someone entering or exiting a room. The point is to make responses active and use action to convey both a sense of an emotional state and the pace of the story. In longer written work like Mills and Boon novels the scenes in the plot plan often rotate the characters at the centre of the action. However, in all of these examples the emphasis is on action, however small, to convey some details of emotional state. Consider the following. The extract comes from a Mills and Boon novel, *Emma And The Earl*. This event closes the second chapter of the story. The character referred to as John is facing the biggest test at this point. In reality he is The Earl Of Palliser. He is pretending to be someone else. The two principal characters are having their first face to face meeting over dinner having corresponded for a long time. Emma is struggling to stay calm through the strong feelings of attraction she has towards John. He feels the same way with the added burden of carrying his deception. The two characters negotiate their way towards a further meeting. In each case their movements and reactions, their active traits, carry much of the important information. Look in particular at John's movements and the final active trait as he breathes out.

"You will come with me, won't you?"

His eyes widened and she could have sworn he said, "Now that would be taking a hell of a chance."

"I beg your pardon?" she asked.

He sipped his wine, then swiped the napkin across his mouth. "I said that would be a good chance to get to know you better."

"So you'll come?"

A corner of his mouth twisted upwards, and he shook his head. "I don't think I'll be able to make it. But you don't need me there."

"Yes I do." She smiled. "It would be so much *fun*. Come on, won't you even consider it?"

"I'll-" he nodded, as if trying to convince someone other than her. "I'll check my schedule, but I can't make any guarantees. Though maybe it would be best if I was there."

She raised an eyebrow. "Best?"

"I mean I know my way around the island a little bit. It might make it a little easier for you."

She smiled. "I'd love it."

"Okay, then." He took a long, deliberate breath and let it out slowly. "I'll see what I can do." [2]

The black moment in a plot plan is often the moment at which the events of the story threaten to overwhelm the main character. Most stories have a black moment. If this moment doesn't threaten to completely overwhelm a character it usually threatens the success of any scheme or plan with which the audience might sympathise. Black moments are an element of most well-known stories including folk tales, jokes and legends. The following example is a well-known traditional story worked into a Christmas Carol. This is a well-defined black moment, it threatens to overwhelm a character and also scupper the success of the mission.

Good King Wenceslas last looked out, on the Feast of Stephen,
When the snow lay round about, deep and crisp and even:
Brightly shone the moon that night, though the frost was cruel,
When a poor man came in sight, gathering winter fuel.

The king is watching the poor peasant gathering fuel in the cold night. He goes on to ask one of his pages if he knows the peasant. The page says he knows the man and knows where he lives. The king and the page head out to deliver meat, wine and logs to the peasant. The night is freezing, the weather bad. The page begins to have doubts. The black moment comes at the start of the fourth verse as the page talks to the king.

Sire the night is darker now, and the wind blows stronger;
Fails my heart I know not how; I can go no longer.

If the page can't go on their mission will be a failure. King Wenceslas tells the page to tread in his footsteps. The final verse runs:

> In his masters steps he trod, where the snow lay dinted;
> Heat was in the very sod, which the saint had printed.
> Therefore Christian men be sure, wealth or rank possessing.
> Ye who now will bless the poor, shall yourselves find blessing.

It is a moral tale, stating the importance self-sacrifice and the need to learn from saintly examples. The saintliness of the king gives the story a twist that takes it out of the realm of the purely physical. However, the five verses are a well-constructed breakdown of a classic narrative and in the character of the page and his struggle through wind and snow we have a character with whom we can identify.

Iconic Moments

Some academic analysis of media work concentrates on iconic moments. The word 'icon' is used loosely to describe images and events that have come to symbolise a time or place. In academic terms the meaning is more precise. To be iconic something has to observe the rules of a 'sign.' Put simply signs must:

i. Be widely used and understood.

ii. Resemble the thing they represent.

iii. Refer to something other than themselves.

In iconic moments there is a marked physical or perceptual resemblance between the signifier (the image we see) and the thing it represents.

Iconic moments are not, as a rule, part of the teaching on courses aimed at popular writing. However, writing that aims for deep meanings benefits from identifying and developing iconic moments. The theoretical aspect of iconic moments makes them hard for some students to grasp. However, considering your own experience of iconic moments as applied to your life and experience of the work of writers makes it obvious that most of us have an instinctive grasp of this point.

Consider the following story told to me by my dad who had heard it from the athlete John Kirkbride. Kirkbride is one of the best athletes ever to come out of West Cumbria. A middle distance runner who represented his country many times including an appearance at the 1972 Olympics in Munich. One day John Kirkbride was training in a typical West Cumbrian downpour with sheeting rain, leaden skies and a cold wind. Running along the bank of a river he passed a fisherman, covered from head to toe in waterproofs and sitting immobile as he watched his float bobbing in the water. The pair looked at each other as Kirkbride sped by. Eventually the fisherman spoke. "Yer mad!" he said.

This may be classic grim West Cumbrian humour but it is also a true story and it fits the description of an iconic moment. The description "mad" for behaviour that seems eccentric or extreme is widely used and understood. Kirkbride running full-tilt in weather that would drive most people indoors resembles the behaviour of a genuinely mad person. In fact, the physical resemblance is clear cut, emphasising the iconic nature of the moment. Finally, the moment and the image refer to something other than themselves. The moment represents an acknowledgement of the link between the two men who had an empathy because they'd chosen pursuits that set them apart from others. It is the kind of moment that might help a person define their own feelings about themselves. Kirkbride was different. To the best of my knowledge he was the only West Cumbrian in the track and field competitors in the Munich Olympic Games.

We all have iconic moments in our lives. Writers concerned with making meaning and making money often develop their iconic moments around the simplest actions in life. For example, couples disagreeing and splitting up often walk away from each other. The current edition of *The Guinness Book Of British Hit Singles* lists four different hit songs called 'Walk Away', and the number of song titles starting with the words 'Walk' and 'Walking' makes a column over one page long in the index including titles like 'Walk Away From Love.' None of which includes a slew of other titles like 'I'm Walking Away.' Pop songs have limited time and wordage to make a point and frequently create scenes in their lyrics which serve as iconic moments. A quick scan of any lyrics you have to hand, printed on a CD insert, will probably present you with some iconic moments based on everyday events.

George Harrison's classic love song opened with a simple and effective observation about:

Something in the way she moves,

In George Harrison's case the song went on to discuss his attraction to Patti Boyd. [3] The same opening six words also form part of a song by James Taylor. In the case of Taylor's song 'Something In the Way She Moves' [4] he goes on to sing a song in praise of a woman who keeps him calm and helps him escape from his troubles. Taylor's song comes from a period in his life which included a short stay in a psychiatric ward.

Both these songs focus on simple actions which could be taken as iconic. Touching and tender observations, but also a reality that most of us can relate to. The people with whom we fall in love and the stories, both triumphant and tragic, we go on to tell have an iconic quality. In some cases these moments revolve around the feeling we had just touching or noticing another person. Well-planned narratives use these everyday events and carefully build in their significance.

One interesting example of this is the gay following for the actress Jodie Foster. Foster belongs to an unusual group of celebrities, claimed as gay by some but never openly admitting to this themselves. [5] Audiences read meanings into the characters played by Foster. One television documentary explored the way the actress had taken on a gay iconography. [6] There is some debate about the intention of film-makers in presenting this aspect to Foster's characters. This is a sensitive issue. One argument suggests Foster is working her way through a career and taking the best roles available. Another argument suggests that film producers and her management, aware of Foster's loyal gay audience, build iconic moments into her movies suggesting a gay reading of her character. In the Channel Four documentary *Celluloid Heroes* a number of film critics and Foster fans discussed such iconic moments in her work. For example, a scene at the opening of *Silence Of The Lambs* [7] in which Foster's character, Clarice Starling, is called to a meeting. As Clarice enters a crowded corridor in the FBI training facility her small and slender body is surrounded by bustling male recruits. She slaps hands with the only other female in the corridor who greets her with a friendly, "Hey, Clarice." The same female trainee will exchange eye contact in a loving way as Clarice passes out of her training at the end of the movie. Clarice walks to the end of the corridor, getting into a lift surrounded by male recruits dressed in bright red. She is dwarfed by them and still wearing her sweaty grey jogging gear. The iconography of these scenes has a particular meaning to Foster's gay following. The brief slapping of hands and the eye contact at the end of the movie can be read as an acknowledgement of the need for some gay people to keep their relationships secret to themselves. The constant opposing of Foster's small female body with groups of large male bodies can be read as a reference to the way the male world appears harsh and uninviting to gay females. Other iconic readings of Foster's characters suggest that the most ordinary actions of her characters might be affected by her sexuality. Foster's brother has discussed her sexuality in terms that might please her gay fans, [8] making them more likely to see these readings as valid.

For writers there is one grim and inescapable truth about iconic moments. The vast majority of such moments we construct will never become totally iconic because the work containing these nuggets will never reach a huge audience. You could see this thought as discouraging or take it as a challenge, resolving to create the best work possible. As Oscar Wilde stated, "We are all of us in the gutter, but some of us are staring at the stars." [9] A useful motto for the situation in which many writers find themselves, working on small scale and achievable targets but aiming for much greater things. In some cases the iconic moment may almost be an accident. For example, Robert De Niro's portrayal of the volatile *Taxi Driver* [10], Travis Bickle, has made De Niro's repeated and menacing line "Are you talkin' to me?" iconic. In reality, De Niro improvised the words and they worked so well that they were left in the final movie. They may have been De Niro's words but the accolades poured onto the original script and direction are still justified. For the actor to be far enough into character to live and act his part this well he required a good script, a clear understanding of his character and the ability to develop this reality under direction.

As a writer it is important you grasp the potential importance of a moment in your work. Some forms of creative work, like cartoons and greetings cards, are conceived as moments. The ability to create such moments can be a lucrative asset to a writer. Elsewhere in scripts, stories and speech-based work there is a place for well-crafted and well-considered iconic moments. The search for meaning and connection with your readers also benefits immeasurably from the ability to focus issues and ideas into a single moment. An iconic moment focuses big issues and ideas to perfection, but character and setting are also vital.

People And Places

Many books on writing spend thousands of words exploring character and setting and considering the implications of decisions made with regard to each. You can learn a great deal from examining the work of others in this regard, and some of the books which devote huge wordage to the issues are outlined at the back of this work. My reason for going over the main points and then setting you an exercise is my own experience that most writers learn effectively about character and setting through their own writing.

Paul Magrs observed in *The Creative Writing Coursebook* that: 'Fiction allows the reader to become the most discreet and the most untraceable of house-breakers.' [11] We as writers go one better. We see the details like rooms and the corners of the character's minds that don't make the final cut. In other words, we understand the decisions and accidents that got our characters and situations into their own particular reality. The reality that our work describes.

I'm aware that, for many of the writers I teach, some sense of place and character is firmly embedded in their minds before we even start work. I once had a student who opened her discussion of her first assignment with the observation that she had turned many of her friends and family into a repertory company for her written stories. My friend, the scriptwriter and playwright Michael Ellis, once told me a story about basing a very unsympathetic character in a stage play on an acquaintance of his. The play opened to good reviews and appreciative audiences, Michael's acquaintance turned up to watch one night, and laughed in all the right places along with the rest of the audience.

The truth is, most of us don't see ourselves exactly as others see us. We also see our surroundings differently, depending on our perspectives. Training for people dealing with the disabled often includes briefly disabling the trainees and obliging them to see an environment from a viewpoint like that of a wheelchair user or blind person.

The exercises so far in this book should have given you a basis from which to develop character and setting in your writing. The observations of people and places, word mimes, conversations with characters and other activities have already started you thinking along these lines. Many of the examples covered so far, from the context and character of Cash Clay, father of Muhammad Ali, to the implicit character of the writers like Thomas Lynch and Sylvia Smith, have shown ways of presenting yourself and others. Similarly, the issue of setting has been explored through examples as diverse as *Monty Python's Meaning Of Life*, the war poem of Wilfred Owen, Simon Armitage's exploration of the north of England and Rebecca Ray's nameless main character observing the state of her home.

It may be useful to glance briefly back over these examples and look at the way that each conveys its own unique sense of character or setting. Before we attempt some more involved work that unites all the elements in this chapter I think it useful to round up some of the advice that is generally imparted about character and setting.

Character: Creating character depends on finding the voice and appearance of a person, or thing. Inanimate objects can be characterful. This is especially obvious in work aimed at children. For example, the enduring and highly profitable Thomas The Tank Engine series has succeeded partly because the railway engines and buses that form the main characters are more realistic and lifelike than the humans. Even the minor characters like Bertie The Bus are more characterful than human characters, many of whom are reduced to their function, for example Thomas' driver. The cars in the *Love Bug* series of movies and the children's favourite *Chitty Chitty Bang Bang* are also characters.

Central characters usually require some element of internal conflict. The classic in this case being Hamlet who, through the appearance of his father's ghost, knows that his father was murdered by his uncle who went on to marry Hamlet's mother and assume the throne as King of Denmark. Hamlet's distaste at the events and speed of the change is represented in a telling line, "The funeral baked meats did coldly furnish the marriage tables," and, eventually in the classic "To be or not to be?" soliloquy. Knowing your character well allows you to create everything from their speech to their clothing in a convincing manner. They can then impose themselves on the world you have created in a way that is likely to carry your audience with them. Characters need a means of identity. This means getting the small details right. If a character is simply the means by which a major point is to be made we run the risk of creating a caricature. For example, Tom Hanks lawyer, dying of AIDS, in the movie *Philadelphia* is all the more effective as a means of portraying the tragedy of the disease because we are dropped into his life as a lawyer, his steady relationship and the love of his family. He is anything but a gay stereotype and the events of his becoming infected with the disease are only unveiled late in the movie. By this time our involvement with the character is well established as he fights his own legal case against his employers.

Don't be afraid of being intrusive with your own characters. Anything, from the way they laugh to their secret love of Sherbet Dips, is engaging and effective when handled properly. Consider the following examples, one factual, one fictional:

The fictional extract comes from *The Piano* by Jane Campion and Kate Pullinger. The opening extract of Ada's story is highly intrusive, allowing us the first privileged insight as readers into a character who will collide with two men and the values of a small rural community. Our understanding of Ada's inner voice, the connection between music and her very soul, and the fact that her silence will inevitably affect others set up the whole story to follow.

> The voice you hear is not my speaking voice.
>
> I have not spoken since I was six years old. No one knows why, not even me. My father says it is a dark talent and the day I take it into my head to stop breathing will be my last.
>
> Today he married me to a man I've not yet met. Soon my daughter and I shall join him in his own country. My husband said my muteness does not bother him. He writes and hark this: God loves dumb creatures, so why not he!

Were good he had God's patience for silence affects everyone in the end. The strange thing is I don't think myself silent, that is, because of my piano. I shall miss it on the journey. [12]

The factual extract comes from *Trials Of The Monkey* by Matthew Chapman. The author, a screenwriter by trade, is a direct descendant of Charles Darwin. He travels to the scene of the infamous Stopes trial in which a teacher was prosecuted for pushing the theories of Darwin over a literal reading of *The Bible*. In his autobiographical book Chapman also heads off in search of himself. An honest, intrusive and characterful passage towards the beginning of the book sets up the self-searching and dark humour that will inform the physical and mental journeys to come. It comes from Chapter 1 which is also called 'The End.'

When Darwin called his second book *The Descent Of Man* instead of *The Ascent Of Man* he was thinking of his progeny. One only has to study the chronology to see the truth of this.

First there was Charles Darwin, two yards long and nobody's fool. Then there was his son, my great-grandfather, Sir Francis Darwin, an eminent botanist. Then came my grandmother, Frances, a modest poet who spent a considerable amount of time in rest-homes for depression. From her issued my beloved mother, Clare, who was extremely short, failed to complete medical school and eventually became an alcoholic.

Then we get down to me. I'm in the movie business. [13]

Setting: The same elements that make character effective may also be applied to setting. Setting generally requires a clear purpose. For example, Thomas The Tank Engine and his friends live and work on the island of Sodor, in reality this island railway system was based on a small railway on The Isle Of Wight. It works wonderfully for children because of the implicit sense that everything is compact and contained. The island retains the feel of a mythical place, like Santa Claus' home in Lapland. Each place is clearly rooted in reality but also touched with a sense of magic and charm. Not exactly the case with the grisly vision of New York contained in movies like *Taxi Driver* and *Flawless* both of which use a city as a receiving station for many who seek anonymity or resort to almost animalistic behaviour.

In other cases the creative use of location is a mix of practicality and creativity. A series of low-budget horror movies have used desert, woodland or other rural settings. Film critics may write long and meaningful studies of the metaphorical aspects of such works but the truth is also that movies like

The Blair Witch Project, The Texas Chainsaw Massacre, The Hills Have Eyes and *The Evil Dead* were produced on budgets so low as to demand the use of free locations and natural light as far as possible. In contrast, the enduring appeal of fantasy and science fiction writing is partly their celebration of the potential of the novel to create any kind of scenery and dispense with the need to adhere strictly to the laws of physics. Robert Rankin has based the most outlandish comedy-fantasy adventures in and around Brentford in London. The Flying Swan pub and several of his friends regularly interact with aliens, vast universal conspiracies and incredible shifts in logic. Their cost on the page is simply the cost of printing any popular novel. Their cost on a cinema screen would put the budgets for the true realisation of Rankin's very unique visions on a par with the budgets for *The Lord Of The Rings* movies.

There are numerous celebrated examples of setting making crucial difference to the success and impact of a particular written work. The Lake District has featured as a location in many written works and Coleridge and Wordsworth amongst others are still celebrated as the lake poets. The following extract comes from the first book of *The Prelude* by Wordsworth. In this extract Wordsworth remembers an incident when, as a schoolboy, he stole out at night and helped himself to a boat before rowing out onto Ullswater.

> One summer evening... I found
> A little boat tied to a willow tree
> Within a rocky cave, its usual home
> Straight I unloosed her chain, and stepping in
> Pushed from the shore.

At first he rows out, enjoying the adventure and taking in the unique sights. His oars disturb the water, leading to a striking image.

> ... did my boat move on.
> Leaving behind her still, on either side
> Small circles glittering idly in the moon,
> Until they melted all into one track
> Of sparkling light

He rows further into the lake and eventually the scenery imposes itself on him to the point that his feelings about boat stealing change.

> ...my boat
> Went heaving through the water like a swan;
> When, from behind a craggy steep till then

The horizon's bound, a huge peak, black and huge,
As if with voluntary power instinct
Upreared its head.

In other words, Wordsworth's journey towards the middle of the lake leads him to see a large mountain top appear from below the horizon. The image of the peak, black against the moonlight sky, strikes him. It appears almost to have a mind of its own and be chasing him across the lake. The extract ends with the poet reflecting on the fright he felt and telling us that the fear stayed with him long afterwards and...

Huge and mighty forms, that do not live
Like living men, moved slowly through the mind
By day, and were a trouble to my dreams. [14]

In less than fifty lines Wordsworth turns Ullswater at night from his own personal domain, an arena fit for the most daring of dreams, into the setting for a horror movie. The description of setting is the key to the transition. The contrasting images of the idle glitter of the disturbance created by his oars and the monstrous peak achieve most of this. But, we are talking about the same place, minutes apart. The point is clear. Setting is what you make it. The places and characters in your writing are under your command.

The speed of Wordsworth's transition is echoed every time you watch a major soap opera. *Eastenders*, for example, is named after the East End of London in which Albert Square is located. In reality, the importance of the setting is its location within a major city. It is a situation the writers regularly use to good effect. A storyline straddling the end of 2001 and early 2002 concerned the character Zoe. Zoe became a teenage runaway after the unearthing of horrific family secrets which revealed that the woman she had taken for an elder sister was really her mother. Zoe's running away saw her on the streets of London, sleeping rough and involved in the grimmest end of the sex trade in central London. Her scenes in this story were contrasted with the recriminations and agonies of her family in Albert Square. A powerful, audience-grabbing storyline was also made possible because the two locations were close, suggesting the story was believable. Zoe's London and the London of Albert Square presented contrasts that highlighted the character's situation. To a certain extent both added character to the scenes.

The notion of a location behaving like a character is central to the work of some writers. Almost all of the significant action in Woody Allen movies for over a quarter of a century has taken place in New York. In other cases the use of setting as character is a practical move. I once wrote a radio play to be performed in a small studio on a limited budget. The 'two-hander' play needed breadth and I achieved what I could by making the two characters very different. However, the settings in a scruffy little house, a farm and a seashore were also chosen to keep the story alive and moving. [15] Each setting was treated very much like an additional character.

So, I've covered people, places and plots. Now it's your turn.

Exercise 8

Use the background information in this chapter to write both of the following:

> i: A short story of between 1500 and 2000 words.

> ii: A radio monologue in which a character tells a story of their life. The monologue should run between 5 and 10 minutes, (estimate 3 words per second for speech).

In both cases follow the rules outlined below:

Plan each work carefully. Start with a plot idea. Build this into scenes in which the main character faces tests and include a black moment in the final scene in which the character's ambition or existence is seriously threatened. Plan at least one iconic moment and make sure that you could explain to anyone who asked how your choice of character(s) and setting supported the point(s) made by your work.

5. Making Money/Making Meaning

'I don't believe in riches but you should see where I live.'

U2, 'God Part II' *Rattle And Hum*

The notion that art and commercial success exist in different worlds still persists in some quarters of the writing world. One school of thought suggests the whole idea is rubbish and that if Shakespeare were alive and well today he would be a highly paid screenwriter. Elsewhere people claim that any truck with the values of an industry that seeks to mass-produce and promote work is a sell-out. I'm not likely to resolve that complex debate in this chapter. I think it important that we acknowledge the differing opinions and I think it important that you decide where you stand. The opinions of others might guide you but the debate about art and commerce is as subjective and intense as any about religion. Your own instinctive feelings on the issue are the most important factor in making sense of the issues covered in this chapter.

Some writing sets out to make money. That much is obvious from the existence of commercial publishers, film studios, greetings card manufacturers and the rest. Some work is less concerned with money. The following poem comes from a collection called *Inside The Outsiders*. The book presents writing from people involved in an outpatient class on creative writing. All of the writers have experienced mental health problems. SH Carter's contributions to the anthology include:

> Reminiscence
> Coasting across fate
> Like a feather in the air
> Lost and found without a care
> Sleepy into slumber
> Solace is my friend
> in her abode too deep to comprehend
> Hazy shapeless mist
> Wells up tumbles down
> Gliding over lightly but never comes around
> Taken into limbo
> Land that time forgot
> Yesterday is over but then maybe not [1]

The poem is a highly personal account, touching on emotions and a struggle for meaning and control. The same issues underpin the story of singer John Otway. His chaotic musical career is the subject of a three times published autobiography. In Otway's case the story is presented at full book length. Despite its highly personal nature the tale has been shaped to explain the most incredible events to a reader who knows nothing about Otway. To this end the book presents both a 'strap line' and 'thumbnail sketch' of events on the cover. A strap line is a one sentence summary of a piece of writing. A thumb nail sketch is a short and punchy description of the complete work. In *Cor Baby That's Really Me!* the two are as follows:

> Strap line: 'Rock and Roll's Greatest Failure!'
>
> Thumbnail: 'Time was when John Otway looked forward to platinum albums, stadium gigs and a squad of bodyguards to see him safely aboard his private jet. Unfortunately, it didn't happen that way.
>
> A series of dreadful career decisions, financial blunders and bad records has left Otway down but not out. This is his story in his own words.
>
> It is the story of a man who...
>
> * Almost rejected Pete Townsend as his producer
>
> * Has never repaid a record company advance in his life
>
> * Once put on a benefit concert for his own record company after they had cancelled his contract
>
> * Signed himself to the mighty Warner Brothers label simply by pressing his own records with the WB logo in the middle, and
>
> * Broke up with Paula Yates, telling her it was the last chance she'd get to go out with a rock star.
>
> *Cor Baby That's Really Me!* is John Otway's hilarious yet moving account of his insane assault on the music industry, a tale of blind ambition and rank incompetence, and a salutary lesson to aspiring musicians on how *not* to achieve greatness - although since this is the third, improved, Millennium edition of this book, with a whole new chapter and pictures of John Otway's gig in the Albert Hall, perhaps success is threatening to break in! [2]

Like SH Carter's poem, Otway's tale is one in which the writer struggles for control and focus only to be thwarted repeatedly. The thumbnail sketch is drawn from the back cover copy. Predictably, it highlights key issues and details in the hope of selling the book to the widest audience.

The two writers are not as far apart as first glances might indicate. John Otway has never been mentally ill but many of the antics in his book border on the truly bizarre. It is possible to draw some similarities of meaning from both writers. However, the contexts are completely different. SH Carter's work is presented in a collection that makes sense when funded with public money and sold at a price that aims to break even. The real purposes of the writing in *Inside The Outsiders* is to provide a therapeutic outlet for the writers themselves and an insight for the rest of us into the experiences of the group.

Otway's autobiography makes a determined effort to draw in a wider readership. It is a commercial venture. Traditionally the publishing decisions relating to musicians' autobiographies start by considering the numbers in their audience, their current profile and their record sales. On almost all of these counts Otway is an unlikely contender for a three times published book. The continuing success of the title is down to a number of things but the strap line 'Rock and Roll's greatest failure,' along with the intriguing stories outlined on the back cover have been helpful. The publicity in magazines and continuing recommendations from readers have kept the book's sales afloat and taken it from a very low-key first publication to a place on the list of a specialist music book company.

Only the two authors could truly tell us how much of their work is invention and how much sincerely represents their own intentions when they started writing. The examples show us the scope available in representing issues of confusion and struggle in life.

Consider the following examples. Once again there are similarities. Both are novels, both have a strong male theme and revolve around gangs of men. Both feature unsuccessful or loser characters in central roles and both tread a narrative line in which issues of morality and the role of the law are complex. Beyond this, the works could not be more different.

John Steinbeck's writing has long been recognised as some of the most telling of the twentieth century. His work often revolves around the lives of struggling Americans. The tales frequently tackle major issues of life from the perspective of the disadvantaged and overlooked. *Tortilla Flat* revolves around Danny, a returnee from World War 1, and his friends. In the preface Steinbeck tells us

> This is the story of Danny and of Danny's friends and Danny's house. It is a story of how these three became one thing... when you speak of Danny's house you are understood to mean a unit

of which the parts are men, from which came sweetness and joy, philanthropy and, in the end, a mystic sorrow.

Steinbeck goes on to compare Danny and his friends to other mythical heroes including Robin Hood and King Arthur and his knights. Chapter 1 opens:

> When Danny came home from the army he learned that he was an heir and an owner of property. The viejo, that is the grandfather, had died leaving Danny the two small houses on Tortilla Flat.

> When Danny heard about it he was a little weighed down with the responsibility of ownership. Before he ever went to look at the property he bought a gallon of red wine and drank most of it himself. The weight of responsibility left him then, and his very worst nature came to the surface.

Danny's worst nature at this stage involves shouting, having fights and breaking a few chairs. Danny gathers friends around him. Their lives take on the duties outlined in the preface. In their own understated way they are wise, philanthropical and crusading. Eventually, the cracks in their alliance appear and Danny dies. The final paragraph of the book hints at the mystic sorrow mentioned in the preface. Danny is dead. His house, on which the lives of Danny and his friends have been centred, is in the final stages of burning down. His friends and neighbours are watching.

> The people of the Flat melted into the darkness. Danny's friends still stood looking at the smoking ruin. They looked at one another strangely, and then back to the burned house. After a while they turned and walked slowly away, and no two walked together. [3]

Steinbeck's writing is precise and accomplished. The author continues to be studied on exam courses in English. He remains in command of his material throughout the book, using the story of a group of men struggling to make a difference in life to explore wider issues of how we make and understand myths. As with Steinbeck's very best work this is a story rich in human qualities. From Danny's drinking in the face of responsibility to the aching sorrow of the final parting, *Tortilla Flat* carries a reader through the lives of flawed but extremely sympathetic characters, asking deep questions about what we all want from life and what it means to be a hero or good person.

76

The same issues inform Stanley Manly's *Raiders Of The Low Forehead*. But the book is unlikely ever to form part of an English course. There is no preface but the first page reads:

> About the author
>
> Stanley Manly wrote this book.

The whole of chapter 1 is contained inside fifty words.

> 01 - Sex
>
> She was hot.
>
> He was randy.
>
> She was easy.
>
> His meat was hard.
>
> She met him on the quay-side when she knocked off work.
>
> She gutted fish, like a real un'.
>
> "Come on," she said, "let's do it."
>
> They did.
>
> Then they went for chips.

From which point the book proceeds to tell an unremitting tale that plumbs the depths of depravity and touches on many taboos. The 45 chapters repeat the titles Sex, Food and Violence in that order 15 times. There is cannibalism, bestiality and some extremely sick humour. In one chapter the hero VINCE EAGER and his girlfriend SHARON GOER repeatedly have sex. At the end of each sex act she keeps trying to remember a word. Their sex doesn't move the plot forward at all. Eventually the lurid sexual encounter ends and she remembers the word:

> "Gratuitous, it's that word I was trying to think of earlier. That word that means something that's just thrown in when there's no need for it. You know... like when you see some couple having sex for ages in a film and it doesn't move the story forward or anything. Gratuitous, that's the word."
>
> "Yeah," agreed VINCE, still stunned at the forceful flood that had ejected itself from his body.

"S'funny," said SHARON, "you get loads of gratuitous sex in movies but you don't see enough of it in books."

The story rages through more gluttony and violence including a dreamed black moment in which VINCE finds himself strapped to a cinema seat watching a movie of every act of masturbation he has committed in his life. In the cinema seats around him are all the girls he was thinking of as he went through these acts. Improbably VINCE succeeds in defeating the bestial trio of *Raiders of the low forehead*. The book ends with the morally good characters in a pub celebrating their unlikely success. The final sentence reads:

And they all lived happily for the next 23 minutes. [4]

Like *Tortilla Flat*, *Raiders Of The Low Forehead* achieved its aims. The book became notorious and attracted scathing reviews from some hardened critics which were then used to promote the work. Like John Otway's book, *Raiders Of The Low Forehead* sold partly on word of mouth recommendations and a reputation generated by a hard-core following.

Tortilla Flat and *Raiders Of The Low Forehead* share few fans and little critical common ground. Their importance in this consideration of money and meaning is that each shows an author striving to achieve a particular effect and using all the skills outlined so far in this book to ensure success. Each book sets up its reality and meaning with a few well-appointed words, each uses well-considered twists and turns of plot to lead the reader and each ends with a telling final sentence that leaves the reader's imagination to outline the story that follows the end of the book.

Tortilla Flat has the financial and critical advantages of being a classic work, studied and read decades after its initial publication. *Raiders Of The Low Forehead* aims for a different kind of profile. It is a cult work and, as such, clearly defines itself as a work outside the mainstream. A success for this book came in the form of a *Times* review saying that '*Raiders Of The Low Forehead* is enough to make a sane person weep.' [5] This might appear to be a complete put-down, but quoting critical comment like this allows the publishers to make the point that it is truly a cult work, shocking enough to be noticed in a market striving for shock value.

We shouldn't be so surprised that John Steinbeck and Stanley Manly are reliant on the same skills because creative writing in all its forms is an art passed down over centuries. Narrative structure was first widely established as an oral tradition in the days when most people could not read and write. We can still see remnants of this fact in modern folk tales like urban legends. One celebrated urban legend concerns an old woman getting into a lift in an upmarket American hotel. She finds a group of tall, black men in suits and dark glasses. Having dragged her case in she hears one of the men say "Hit the ground," at which point she dives flat on her face. The lift reaches the ground, the men walk out, the embarrassed woman picks herself up and heads for the checkout desk. When she tries to pay her bill the manager tells her there is no need because it has already been settled. He then hands her a note that says, 'Thanks for the best laugh I've had in years. Yours Eddie Murphy.'

This story is provably an urban legend. It has appeared in collections of such stories and the same story continually circulates with key details, like the location of the hotel and the name of the famous black man, changing. I've heard versions of the story that use Richard Pryor, Mike Tyson and Will Smith in place of Murphy. I've also heard one report that the story goes back to the 1960s and names Cassius Clay.

Urban legends often deal with our deepest fears or articulate issues that are hard to discuss in other ways. The legend above says a lot about racial tensions that exist to this day and the kind of mistaken assumptions people continually make. It also follows a clear narrative pattern and delivers a surprising message. Most narrative writing, whether it be for scripts, novels or songs, follows a pattern we naturally adopt in our own thoughts. We identify opportunities and possibilities, make decisions and follow the results to their conclusions. It is the means, crudely, by which narrative fiction is constructed.

Poetry has a similar overlap to everyday life. Much poetic association and most commonly used literary devices in poetry have their roots in real life. One danger of over-analysing creative work is that we concentrate so much on the work that we lose touch with these important roots.

People frequently compare and contrast, liken other people and things to totally unrelated objects and think in symbolic ways. Even people who deny the latter can report bizarre dreams indicating that their minds create poetic allusions. The same skills of invention and creativity that inform the most ambitious poetry also find other applications. Consider the following examples:

> Monkshood
> Suitably darker tones than indigo,
> a thunder sky reflected in a lake
> roofed over by dense trees. Our high ladder
> lost legs after you went too far
> and dropped the glass word we had kept
> hidden for future retrieval.

A curtain's drawn across the horizon
each time I contemplate a life
without you as its centre. When I hear
the singer a-capella, and the note
is bruised, but hits the purple spot,
I think of monkshood or bitter coffee
stripping defence by its scent,
I let go, and a road leads dustily
towards a house stepped back from a quarry
from which occasionally someone appears
carrying a thought in their hands
that's busy like an animal.
Dark tone again. The black petunia
a tortoise bites in a garden, and now
a clearer indicator, words that beat
persistently at paper walls, and break
sense barriers. I close my eyes, count three,
the flowers take a breather in the hall.

                                        Jeremy Reed

In recent years a series of black and white commercials have been filmed
to advertise Guinness. Showing in cinemas and on television the series has
developed a theme that praises people who wait, think deeply and find
meanings in places others do not consider looking. The commercials have
included the famous winner of a poll on the best adverts ever made. The 'he
waits' commercial featured a surfer waiting for the perfect wave. Other
commercials have centred on an annual challenge to swim a circuit around a
coastal harbour and the followers of snail racing. One commercial built
around a dream sequence featured a human tower in which one man struggled to the top and looked through a hole in a wall only to be confronted
with a vision of himself, slumped face down asleep on a bar-room table. At
this point the man started laughing insanely and woke up. Those around him
struggled to understand what was going on.

Although Jeremy Reed and the Guinness commercials might not find the
same audience they do give us some useful insights into the issues of meaning and money. In both cases the work relies on a combination of highly
personal interpretations of meaning, based on observations of life we can all
share. "Monkswood" is an intense and personal poem rich in images and
references, suggesting meanings related to the poet and his lost love:

When I hear
the singer a-capella, and the note
is bruised, but hits the purple spot,
I think of monkshood or bitter coffee

Elsewhere the imagery may be personal but it also works to convey a mood and a sense of the poet's situation.

a thunder sky reflected in a lake
roofed over by dense trees.

The poem is a journey into personal experience. It draws in the reader through a combination of meditative observations and creative inventions. Amongst the latter we find:

words that beat
persistently at paper walls, and break
sense barriers.

By contrast the Guinness commercials aim their creative thrust outwards. They create a generality, a world in which it is suggested that certain people might share a viewpoint. Another difference between the commercials and the poem is the suggestion in the commercials that there are values to which we might aspire. The famous 'he waits' commercial is the best example of this. It opened the account and set an identity that could be explored in the later adverts.

The inventive use of imagery unites both works. In both cases we have imagery that includes the very personal, like the dream-based commercial or the references to coffee and monkswood. Both works are also united by the fact that they were seen to make financial sense, although in this aspect the decisions were very different.

Some of Jeremy Reed's work including 'Monkswood' is published by Crescent Moon. Their entry in the *Writers Handbook* says the following: 'FOUNDED 1988 to publish critical studies of figures such as DH Lawrence, Thomas Hardy...' The entry lists a range of eminent figures including writers and artists. It continues '*Publishes* literature, criticism, media, art, feminism, painting, poetry, travel, guidebooks, cinema and some fiction. Literary magazine *Passion* launched February 1994.'

The company publish '15-20' titles each year and request aspiring writers not to send complete manuscripts in the first instance. They prefer writers to 'approach in writing first and send an s.a.e.' [7] Crescent Moon's profitability rests on the existence of a loyal audience for high quality and inventive writing. Companies like Crescent Moon have increased sales with the growth of the Internet because their dedicated audience will take the trouble to seek out and buy the work of writers like Jeremy Reed. The falling costs of production linked to the widening availability and increasing power of information technology have also proven an asset to small publishers. A good selling title for such a company would shift several hundred copies netting modest but welcome profits for author and publisher. Operations like Crescent Moon are a major part of the reason that the standard reference works *The Writers And Artists Yearbook* and *The Writers Handbook* increase in size every year.

The financial decisions in the case of the Guinness commercials are totally different. Their inventive plots and the quality imbued into every aspect of the work is the result of a lengthy and expensive process. The understanding from the start is that this work is aimed at an audience of millions with the intention of maintaining the product's jealously guarded position as Britain's most popular brand of bottled beer. The creativity of the work has gained this series of commercials intense respect but, in the end, the decision to make the adverts rested on a series of business meetings between client and agency. Major advertising agencies are organised in a way that allows the inventive thinkers, known as 'creatives,' to work to their strengths whilst others, known as 'account handlers,' work as go-betweens explaining the clients' needs to the creatives and explaining the inventive ideas to the clients.

The examples used so far in the chapter make it clear that the dividing line between creative writing and commercial writing is nowhere near as sharp as many would suggest. Some of the most lucrative writing retains a strong creative element. JK Rowling's Harry Potter books have earned critical respect because of the inventiveness and life in Rowling's writing. The characters and plot devices are without doubt the result of clear creative thinking. The books were not written to fit a formula or existing demand with a publisher. Similarly, the scripting of soap operas, whilst written to fit running times and production demands, manages to evoke genuine insight into people through the creative thinking of the writers. In the year 2001 Jack and Vera Duckworth in *Coronation Street* celebrated 44 years of marriage. Jack, famous for his lack of romance, organised surprises for his wife including a lovingly prepared breakfast and cocktails in his potting shed. It was a celebrated and popular storyline that allowed the couple to represent some deep and touching aspects of a long-term relationship. *Coronation Street* may be a mass-market soap that attracts massive income to the ITV network through the sales of lucrative advertising but to retain audience appeal it needs to be inventive and insightful in the delivery of plot lines. Above all, it is essential that the characters retain their humanity and their ability to remain credible for the viewers. By contrast, it is possible that the most heartfelt and personal writing - work that aims for nothing other than creative insight - might leave many readers completely baffled or indifferent. It is an old adage in Media Studies that audiences give meaning to a work.

Basic Points On Meaning

Most of this book has explored skills and examples that help writers to build meaning into their work. The vast majority of creative writing aims to develop meaning or produce work that, on reflection, might reveal meaning. There is no one set of rules for the production of meaning. All the aspects of writing, from poetic devices to figures of speech, have arisen because they add nuances to the use of language. English is identified as a progressive language because it allows for such developments. Gangsta Rap music which started in the USA shows one aspect of such developments. Rappers reclaimed words which had previously served as terms of abuse and used them in a confrontational and positive way. One demonstration of this was the invention of new spellings, like 'Gangsta,' for old words. One rapper, Tupac, took the reclamation further by turning the word NIGGA into an acronym and translating it, (Never Ignorant, Getting Goals Accomplished).

If your goal on finishing the book revolves mainly around the improvement of your ability to develop and explore meaning through your work the following approaches might be useful:

i. Equip yourself with some standard reference works on the English language. I recommend *The Penguin Dictionary Of Literary Terms And Literary Theory* [8] as the best possible start. This work acts as a reference for all manner of literary terms, explaining how literary devices operate and examining the origin, history and meaning of a range of terms like 'Ivory Tower.' Another useful book, not generally used on writing courses, is Raymond Williams' *Keywords* [9]. This is a more modern and specific analysis of terms and ideas that are crucial to our current understanding of the world. Use works gathered in this way as source material in whatever writing work you decide to do. You can attempt writing as short pieces designed to develop some literary device, for example a sonnet. You may also use the reference works to aid your understanding of any other critical material you read. Some reference sources are outlined in a section at the end of this chapter.

ii. Consider other options for developing your work. The obvious move, after having practised your skills for a while, is to join a group of people with a similar interest. Creative writing courses vary enormously and it is advisable to check on the focus of any group before you join. Most groups work in ways that allow writers to explore themes and develop their own talent in a supportive environment. Such group practices allow you to develop your own awareness of how and why you create meanings by putting your work up for discussion in the group.

Basic Points On Money

If you wish to be paid for your writing it is likely that you will become involved in a complex and changing world that you will never totally understand. The good news, however, has already been covered. There is more paid work for writers now than at any time in history and the amount and variety of work continues to increase. Writing for money generally revolves around a number of set situations and this section covers the most basic of ground rules to help you survive.

Much paid work revolves around pre-prepared briefs and contracts in which your creative talent may find a role. In such situations it is almost always advisable to treat the briefs and contracts with respect as most of the people paying you will be experienced and clear about the goals to be achieved. Many writers distrust such rigidity and regard paid employment of this kind as stifling of creativity but, as we have seen, the opportunity to do inventive work that will stretch your abilities does exist. There are pressures but also great rewards for scriptwriters, advertising creatives and others.

Many jobs in this line are never advertised and the best means of becoming employed as a regular writer of material is to actively target the people for whom you wish to work. Methodical approaches are the likeliest means of success. Reference works like *The Writers And Artists Yearbook* and *The Writers Handbook* are ready-made self-help guides, generally giving specific advice and a massive array of contacts. Some areas of employment, for example writing greetings cards, are less well advertised although companies like Emotional Rescue do send out guidelines to aspiring writers. In these cases the best method of gaining employment is to take addresses from the products themselves, make focused and specific approaches and pay attention to what you are told when your phone calls, e-mails and letters are returned.

The most important factor to grasp, and often the hardest aspect of writing for money, is the ability to see your work as others see it. Editors and other employers of writers all struggle to make people see that bright ideas alone are seldom enough. The world is full of people with ideas, people who are funny around pub tables and people who think they should write. That a minority of such people become paid writers says everything about the difficulty of grasping the fact that this is a job like any other. Most publishers, radio production companies and others who can offer work have clear ideas of what they want from unsolicited contributors. Most are deluged with work that indicates that many writers don't pay attention when companies and organisations explain their areas of interest in *The Writers Handbook*, on their websites or wherever else they seek to make themselves known. Some publishers, like Pocket Essentials, take the trouble to outline everything from required wordage to the terms of their contracts on the Internet. When your potential employers have been this forthcoming there is little percentage in offering them anything twice as long as they require simply because you think it a work of genius. Similarly, many publishers have an editorial line that explains itself if you look carefully.

Crescent Moon published Jeremy Reed's poem print 'some fiction,' however, if you offer a novel like *Raiders Of The Low Forehead* you are wasting your time with this company. Their reliance on work of high literary merit and critical studies makes it obvious that their expertise, and most importantly their reliable customers, would not be the likely market for a novel that pushed barriers of taste.

Every time you approach a publisher, television company, film production company or any other producer of your work you are, in effect, asking them to invest their money and reputation in your idea. It is vital to see this request from the perspective of those you are targeting. One consistent mistake that writers make is to assume that bright ideas will be seen for what they are. A great many successful approaches for publication or production finally make the grade after a negotiation. This is why it is important to understand what the people you target might want, and listen to any feedback they give. Above all, it is important that you can explain, defend and change your work if necessary.

A good practice to develop with complicated ideas is to be able to produce a strap line, a short thumbnail sketch of your idea and some idea of what you as a writer bring to the work. This final aspect is sometimes called the writer's voice. Crudely, this equates to being able to explain what you are saying and how you are saying it. Since it is quite likely that complex work will be discussed and modified before being commissioned it is vital that you can hold up your part of any negotiation. An inability to do so could cost you a contract or land you a contract you will struggle to fill.

The financial details of most deals, even those negotiated amicably, represent a power relationship. In most cases the bulk of the power remains with the producer who has earned this position through their building of an operation that makes money by selling work. In some cases, notably those of novels or scripts seeking the approval of large organisations, writers are obliged to go through agents. Agents act as intermediaries. They have more contacts and market knowledge than most writers, along with a working relationship with many in the industry. Agents typically take a percentage, anything from 10% to 25%, of the income from a piece of work. Reputable agents appear in standard reference works and state the percentages they collect in their entries along with details of the kind of work typically handled by their agency.

And Finally

The final point brings us almost full circle to the start of the book. The future direction of your writing is entirely your decision. In the opening chapter I told you, 'Creative writing as a subject can offer you a great deal. It will offer you the most if you are honest with yourself about your own aims.' I hope that the knowledge and insights covered over the course of the last 35,000 words have helped you to find out more about your own abilities. I can't overstate the importance of being honest with yourself.

Writing is an art. As such it obliges us to stretch our skills and abilities, sometimes to breaking point. When you add the financial dimension you also find yourself pitting your skills against the demands of markets and the opinions of those you hope will invest in your talent. It can be a frustrating and bitter experience. It will be less so if your own aims are clear and you treat your writing in a way that consistently convinces you of the progress you are making. When you see a purpose to the activities involved it is more likely you will find the motivation to continue.

One reason I like the line from U2's 'God Part II' which opens this chapter is that it hints clearly at a self-awareness in Bono, who wrote the lyric. It appears to state that creativity and commerce both matter. It also hints at a certain amount of self-depreciating humour. Taken literally the message seems to be that money isn't everything but it does offer satisfaction of a kind. I can't make your decisions for you but I would suggest that Bono's attitude is worth considering. In the end your writing is your work, produced from your decisions and talent. Any other writing isn't exclusively yours. Valuing your work purely on its market value will always open up the possibility that you will be frustrated because of decisions taken by others. However, it is equally narrow-minded to assume that all commercially angled work is a sell-out. It may be true that some huge selling work, including *Harry Potter And The Philosopher's Stone* found rejection before success. Some ground-breaking million-seller books including *M.A.S.H.*, *Dune* and *Jonathan Livingstone Seagull* ran up rejections well into double figures before being published. [10] However, these examples prove only the vagaries of a commercial world that tries to second-guess the market place. They don't indicate that every work rejected by publishers and producers is a gem. Ultimately your writing has to work for you and represent your best efforts. If it surprises, excites and informs you your writing has already done an important job. If it does the same for others in the way you intend you can count yourself truly lucky.

Exercise 9

Review your notes from Exercise 1 and decide for yourself if any important aspect of your intentions about writing has changed.

Decide carefully on your next move as a writer. Consider the following:

Targeting established markets for stories, scripts or other creative developments of ideas.

Joining a writers group or course.

Dedicating yourself to developing one aspect of your work, for example poetry.

Whatever you decide, use the advice here and take time to study anything else you find useful. Some suggested reading is included at the end of this book. There is no substitute for networking, listening carefully to the advice of those who have done the kind of work you aspire to do and putting yourself in situations that allow for feedback on your work. When it comes to writing the world is not short of people with raw talent and ideas. The ability to shape this talent into work that truly inspires and communicates is, however, at a premium.

This is a book about you. In the final reckoning your decisions about your writing will be the most important in determining the course of your work and the level of impact you make on the world.

Notes

Introduction: Pipe Dream Or Practical Subject?

1. Haiku is a 17-syllable form typically presented as lines of five, seven and five syllables in which two elements, typically an image and reflective thought, are presented. The two are divided by a *kireji* or cutting word although this is often reduced to punctuation in English translations of the form. Basho generally wrote rigidly within the form but he did produce work that stepped outside in approach and the number of syllables.

   Matsuo Kinsaku (1644-94) took the surname Basho in honour of a tree given to him by a disciple. Arguably the greatest haiku poet in history, Basho wrote over 1000 of the 17-syllable verses leaving a legacy that reinvigorated and reinvented the form which was in danger of becoming moribund. Basho's work leaned heavily on the concept of 'muga,' literally an identification with the writer's subject matter in which the writer and subject become one. In this context his work offered revelation and reflection on life and established for all time the role of haiku as a meditative form providing a path to enlightened thinking. His work is also notable for a high degree of both simplicity and humour. His greatest haiku are collected in *On Love And Barley: Haiku Of Basho* (Penguin Classics, 1985).

2. Wilfred Owen, *Dulce et decorum est,* in *Early Twentieth-Century Poetry* (Penguin Popular Poetry, 1995), pp 62-63.

3. Work on finding your voice as a writer is a staple of creative writing books and courses. Crudely, your 'voice' is what you say and your own unique way of saying it.

4. Stephen King, *On Writing: A Memoir* (Hodder & Stoughton, 2000), p 77.

5. Oxford Popular English Dictionary (Oxford University Press, 1999), p 534.

1. Seeds

1. The extract printed is a paraphrase of a regular part of Hicks' act. He varied the words but kept the sense of this introduction over many shows. One version of the introduction opens the CD *Philosophy: The Best Of Bill Hicks* (Rykodisc, 2001).
2. *Downs Mail*, December 2001, p 38.
3. Roddy Doyle, *Paddy Clarke Ha Ha Ha* (Reed Audio, 1994).
4. A soliloquy is a solo speech delivered by a character in front of the audience. The best known example is probably Hamlet's "To be or not to be" speech.
5. Davis Miller, *The Tao Of Muhammad Ali* (Vintage, 1996). First section of copy from inside front cover, second section of copy from inside back cover.
6. Rebecca Ray, *A Certain Age* (Penguin, 1998), extracts in order, p 2, p 3, p 12, p 43.
7. Mark Kram, *Ghosts Of Manila* (CollinsWillow, 2001), pp 65-66.

2. Journeys And Migrations

1. Julian Birkett, *Word Power: A Guide To Creative Writing* (A and C Black, 1983), p 15.
2. 'The Site That Is Bringing Home Entertainment To Millions,' *The Independent*, 26 September 1997, p 7.
3. Eibhlin Conroy, *Alcock And Brown* from Erin Gibbons (ed) *Hidden Conamara* (Conamara West Press, 1991), p 27.
4. Sylvia Smith, *Misadventures* (Canongate Press, 2001), p 109.
5. Maya Angelou, *Even The Stars Look Lonesome* (Virago, 1998), p 139.
6. 'A Life Less Ordinary,' *The Independent Review*, 12 March 2001, pp 1 & 7.
7. Julia Bell and Paul Magrs (eds), *The Creative Writing Coursebook* (Macmillan, 2001), p 9.
8. Mark Twain, *The Adventures Of Tom Sawyer* (Penguin Classics, 1994), p 7.
9. Graham Rawle, *More Lost Consonants* (Fourth Estate, 1992), no. 48.

3. Me, Myself And I

1. Simon Armitage, *All Points North* (Penguin, 1999), p 1.
2. Armitage, p 13.
3. Armitage, p 16.
4. Paul Mills, *Writing In Action* (Routledge, 1996), 'Autobiographical Writing,' pp 41-66.
5. Nicci Gerrard, 'Facing The Final Taboo,' *W*, Spring 1997, p 5.
6. Sherwin B Nuland, *How We Die* (Vintage, 1997), pp 157-8.
7. Thomas Lynch, *The Undertaking* (Jonathan Cape, 1997), pp 3-15.
8. Bert Keizer, *Dancing With Mr D.* (Black Swan, 1997), pp 168 & 291-292.
9. Metaphor: 'A figure of speech in which one thing is described as another.' Simile: 'A figure of speech in which one thing is likened to another, in such a way as to clarify and enhance an image.' *Penguin Dictionary Of Literary Terms And Literary Theory: Third Edition* (Penguin, 1992), pp 542 & 880.
10. Monty Python, *Monty Python's Meaning Of Life* (Methuen, 1983). Extracts from 'The Meaning Of Life Part vii, Death.'

4. People, Places And Plots

1. *BBC Drama, Entertainment & Children's Programmes: Writing Drama For BBC Radio And Television, Guidelines For Unsolicited Work*, BBC, 25 May 2001, p 7. The BBC operates a New Writing Initiative to 'target and nurture new writing talent.' Write to New Writing Co-ordinator at: writersroom, Room 222, BBC Broadcasting House, Portland Place, London W1A 1AA. Phone 0207-765-0756.
2. Elizabeth Harbison, *Emma And The Earl* (Mills And Boon Tender Romance, 1999), pp 38-39. Mills and Boon guidelines are available on request from Harlequin Mills and Boon Ltd, Eton House, 18-24 Paradise Road, Richmond, Surrey TW9 1SR. Phone 0208-288-2800, www.millsandboon.co.uk.
3. The Beatles, 'Something,' *Abbey Road* (Apple, 1969).
4. James Taylor, 'Something In The Way She Moves,' *James Taylor* (Apple, 1969).
5. 'Cupboard Love,' *The Independent: 24Seven*, 30 August 1996, p 13.
6. *Celluloid Icons*, Channel 4, 1 September 1996.
7. *The Silence Of The Lamb*s (Columbia Tristar, 1991).
8. Buddy Foster, *Foster Child* (Arrow, 1998), pp 165-170.
9. Oscar Wilde, a quote recently commemorated in a statue dedicated to the poet near Charing Cross Railway Station.

10. *Taxi Driver* (Columbia, 1976).

11. Julia Bell and Paul Magrs (Eds), *The Creative Writing Coursebook* (Macmillan, 2001), p 169.

12. Jane Campion and Kate Pullinger, *The Piano* (Bloomsbury, 1994), p 3.

13. Matthew Chapman, *Trials Of The Monkey* (Duck Editions, 2000), p 5.

14. William Wordsworth, *The Prelude Book 1,* 'A Boat On Ullswater,' this version extracted from: Norman Nicholson. *The Lake District* (Penguin, 1977), pp 98-99.

15. Neil Nixon, *Driftwood*, Oneword Radio, 2002.

5. Making Money/Making Meaning

1. SH Carter 'Reminiscence' from Margaret O'Neill (ed), *Inside The Outsiders* (Park Crescent Writers, 2001), p 32. Available £3 from Park Crescent Writers Group, Park Crescent Centre, Erith Hospital, Park Crescent, Erith, Kent DA8 3EE.

2. John Otway, *Cor Baby, That's Really Me!* (Cherry Red Books, 1998), cover copy.

3. John Steinbeck, *Tortilla Flat* (Heinemann, 1935), extracts p 9, p 17 and p 317.

4. Stanley Manly, *Raiders Of The Low Forehead* (Attack, 1999), extracts p 4, p 5, p 131 and p 152.

5. 'Slash And Burn,' *The Times*: *Metro*, 6 November 1999, p 21.

6. Jeremy Reed, *Brigitte's Blue Heart* (Crescent Moon, 1998).

7. Barry Turner (ed), *The Writers Handbook 2002* (Macmillan, 2001), p 178 & info@crescentmoon.org.uk

8. JA Cuddon & CE Preston (eds), *The Penguin Dictionary Of Literary Terms And Literary Theory* (Penguin, 2000).

9. Raymond Williams, *Keywords* (Fontana, 1988).

10. Older classics rejected over a dozen times include James Joyce's *Dubliners,* turned down 22 times, and the 18-times rejected *Lorna Doone.*

Further Reading

Standard Reference Books

Anyone truly serious about writing is well advised to buy one of the following regularly:

Barry Turner (ed), *The Writers Handbook* (Macmillan, annual publication). An indispensable reference for writers. Exemplary sections on most areas of employment including informed articles on everything from courses to becoming a published poet.

The Writers And Artists Yearbook (A & C Black, annual publication). Longer established than *The Writers Handbook* and aimed at a wider market with much more on the visual arts than the Macmillan title.

Books On Creative Writing

Julia Bell and Paul Magrs (eds), *The Creative Writing Coursebook* (Macmillan, 2001). A compilation of observations and ideas from people involved in teaching on the highly successful creative writing programme at the University Of East Anglia, Norwich. Strong on insight and brave enough to include occasionally contradictory views of the same issues.

Julian Birkett, *Word Power* (A & C Black, 1998). Third edition of a creative writing classic. Erudite, confident and full of useful exercises to develop talent and focus. A standard tool of many creative writing classes.

Carole Blake, *From Pitch To Publication* (MacMillan, 1999). For those intending to turn the craft into the most lucrative writing. A top agent tells you how to write best-selling novels. Pragmatic and well ordered. Like Stephen King's book, credible because of the pedigree of the writer. More of a focussed reference work than a thumping good read but invaluable if read in sections whilst fired up with ambition and imagination.

Dianne Doubtfire, *Teach Yourself Creative Writing* (Hodder & Stoughton, 1983 & 1996). A basic introduction with exercises and separate sections on forms of writing. The exercises and most of the advice on writing are useful. Elsewhere the original 20-year-old manuscript creaks badly. A section on 'Tools Of The Trade' opens with the words 'You will, of course, need a typewriter.' This factor alone was enough to gain one of my students a refund from a bookshop.

Stephen King, *On Writing* (Hodder & Stoughton, 2000). Punchier and less pedantic than most works on the subject. In reality part autobiography and part meditation on the craft. Above all, readable, engaging and sympathetic to the struggles of aspiring writers.

Christopher Vogler, *The Writer's Journey* (Boxtree, 1998). Mythic structure for storytellers and a work that retains an almost mystical hold over aspiring screenwriters. Opinion is sharply divided over the book. A series of fawning five star reviews from readers on the book's Amazon page prove Vogler's advice has been positively life affirming to many.

In addition it is worth studying the lists of some publishers who specialise in works on writing. A & C Black publish a selection of specialist help guides for writers. America's Focal Press publish a comprehensive series of books on professional aspects of writing, like journalism.

The Essential Library: Best-Sellers

Build up your library with new titles every month

Film Noir by Paul Duncan

The laconic private eye, the corrupt cop, the heist that goes wrong, the femme fatale with the rich husband and the dim lover - these are the trademark characters of Film Noir. This book charts the progression of the Noir style as a vehicle for film-makers who wanted to record the darkness at the heart of American society as it emerged from World War to the Cold War. As well as an introduction explaining the origins of Film Noir, seven films are examined in detail and an exhaustive list of over 500 Films Noirs are listed.

Alfred Hitchcock by Paul Duncan

More than 20 years after his death, Alfred Hitchcock is still a household name, most people in the Western world have seen at least one of his films, and he popularised the action movie format we see every week on the cinema screen. He was both a great artist and dynamite at the box office. This book examines the genius and enduring popularity of one of the most influential figures in the history of the cinema!

Orson Welles by Martin Fitzgerald

The popular myth is that after the artistic success of *Citizen Kane* it all went downhill for Orson Welles, that he was some kind of fallen genius. Yet, despite overwhelming odds, he went on to make great Films Noirs like *The Lady From Shanghai* and *Touch Of Evil*. He translated Shakespeare's work into films with heart and soul (*Othello*, *Chimes At Midnight*, *Macbeth*), and he gave voice to bitterness, regret and desperation in *The Magnificent Ambersons* and *The Trial*. Far from being down and out, Welles became one of the first cutting-edge independent film-makers.

Woody Allen (Revised & Updated Edition) by Martin Fitzgerald

Woody Allen: Neurotic. Jewish. Funny. Inept. Loser. A man with problems. Or so you would think from the characters he plays in his movies. But hold on. Allen has written and directed 30 films. He may be a funny man, but he is also one of the most serious American film-makers of his generation. This revised and updated edition includes *Sweet And Lowdown* and *Small Time Crooks*.

Stanley Kubrick by Paul Duncan

Kubrick's work, like all masterpieces, has a timeless quality. His vision is so complete, the detail so meticulous, that you believe you are in a three-dimensional space displayed on a two-dimensional screen. He was commercially successful because he embraced traditional genres like War (*Paths Of Glory*, *Full Metal Jacket*), Crime (*The Killing*), Science Fiction (*2001*), Horror (*The Shining*) and Love (*Barry Lyndon*). At the same time, he stretched the boundaries of film with controversial themes: underage sex (*Lolita*); ultra violence (*A Clockwork Orange*); and erotica (*Eyes Wide Shut*).

The Essential Library: Recent Releases

Build up your library with new titles every month

Tim Burton by Colin Odell & Michelle Le Blanc

Tim Burton makes films about outsiders on the periphery of society. His heroes are psychologically scarred, perpetually naive and childlike, misunderstood or unintentionally disruptive. They upset convential society and morality. Even his villains are rarely without merit - circumstance blurs the divide between moral fortitude and personal action. But most of all, his films have an aura of the fairytale, the fantastical and the magical.

French New Wave by Chris Wiegand

The directors of the French New Wave were the original film geeks - a collection of celluloid-crazed cinéphiles with a background in film criticism and a love for American auteurs. Having spent countless hours slumped in Parisian cinémathèques, they armed themselves with handheld cameras, rejected conventions, and successfully moved movies out of the studios and on to the streets at the end of the 1950s.

Borrowing liberally from the varied traditions of film noir, musicals and science fiction, they released a string of innovative and influential pictures, including the classics *Jules Et Jim* and *A Bout De Souffle*. By the mid-1960s, the likes of Jean-Luc Godard, François Truffaut, Claude Chabrol, Louis Malle, Eric Rohmer and Alain Resnais had changed the rules of film-making forever.

Bollywood by Ashok Banker

Bombay's prolific Hindi-language film industry is more than just a giant entertainment juggernaut for 1 billion-plus Indians worldwide. It's a part of Indian culture, language, fashion and lifestyle. It's also a great bundle of contradictions and contrasts, like India itself. Thrillers, horror, murder mysteries, courtroom dramas, Hong Kong-style action gunfests, romantic comedies, soap operas, mythological costume dramas... they're all blended with surprising skill into the musical boy-meets-girl formula of Bollywood. This vivid introduction to Bollywood, written by a Bollywood scriptwriter and media commentator, examines 50 major films in entertaining and intimate detail.

Mike Hodges by Mark Adams

Features an extensive interview with Mike Hodges. His first film, *Get Carter*, has achieved cult status (recently voted the best British film ever in *Hotdog* magazine) and continues to be the benchmark by which every British crime film is measured. His latest film, *Croupier*, was such a hit in the US that is was re-issued in the UK. His work includes crime drama (*Pulp*), science-fiction (*Flash Gordon* and *The Terminal Man*), comedy (*Morons From Outer Space*) and watchable oddities such as *A Prayer For The Dying* and *Black Rainbow*. Mike Hodges is one of the great maverick British filmmakers.

The Essential Library: Currently Available

Film Directors:

Woody Allen (2nd)	Tim Burton	Ang Lee
Jane Campion*	John Carpenter	Joel & Ethan Coen (2nd)
Jackie Chan	Steven Soderbergh	Clint Eastwood
David Cronenberg	Terry Gilliam*	Michael Mann
Alfred Hitchcock (2nd)	Krzysztof Kieslowski*	Roman Polanski
Stanley Kubrick (2nd)	Sergio Leone	Oliver Stone
David Lynch	Brian De Palma*	George Lucas
Sam Peckinpah*	Ridley Scott (2nd)	James Cameron
Orson Welles (2nd)	Billy Wilder	
Steven Spielberg	Mike Hodges	

Film Genres:

Blaxploitation Films	Bollywood	French New Wave
Horror Films	Spaghetti Westerns	Vietnam War Movies
Slasher Movies	Film Noir	German Expressionist Films
Vampire Films*	Heroic Bloodshed*	Hammer Films

Film Subjects:

Laurel & Hardy	Marx Brothers	Film Music
Steve McQueen*	Marilyn Monroe	The Oscars® (2nd)
Filming On A Microbudget	Bruce Lee	Writing A Screenplay
Film Studies		

TV:

Doctor Who

Literature:

Cyberpunk	Philip K Dick	The Beat Generation
Agatha Christie	Sherlock Holmes	Noir Fiction*
Terry Pratchett	Hitchhiker's Guide (2nd)	Alan Moore
William Shakespeare	Creative Writing	

Ideas:

Conspiracy Theories	Nietzsche	UFOs
Feminism	Freud & Psychoanalysis	Bisexuality

History:

Alchemy & Alchemists	The Crusades	The Black Death
Jack The Ripper	The Rise Of New Labour	Ancient Greece
American Civil War	American Indian Wars	Witchcraft

Miscellaneous:

The Madchester Scene	Stock Market Essentials	Jethro Tull
How To Succeed As A Sports Agent		
How To Succeed In The Music Business		

Available at all good bookstores or send a cheque (payable to 'Oldcastle Books') to:
Pocket Essentials (DeptCWR), 18 Coleswood Rd, Harpenden, Herts, AL5 1EQ, UK.
£3.99 each (£2.99 if marked with an *). For each book add 50p postage & packing in the UK and £1 elsewhere.